The Advanced Book of CAKE DECORATING

The Advanced Book of CAKE DECORATING

Sylvia Coward

NEW HOLLAND

ACKNOWLEDGEMENTS

My thanks to my husband, Vic, for his support, to my
daughters, Shelley, who designed Santa's sleigh on page 94
and for her constructive suggestions and constant support,
and Jenny for her encouragement and long-distance
assistance with typing via the word processor, and to Joana
Nkosi and Sarah Rammushi for their help.

All cake decorating tools, equipment, supplies and special
ingredients by courtesy of THE SUGAR ART SHOP, Edenvale.

First published in the UK in 1991 by
New Holland (Publishers) Ltd
37 Connaught Street, London W2 2AZ

ISBN 1 85368 123 7

Managing Editor: Alison Leach
Editor: Dulcie Andrews
Designer: Jo Tapper
Illustrations: Stuart Perry
Photography: Hilda Kwan
Phototypeset by Bookworm Typesetters, Manchester
Reproduction by P&W Graphics Pte Ltd, Singapore
Printed and bound in Singapore by Tien Wah Press (Pte) Ltd

Contents

Introduction

Even the most experienced cake decorators find that they never stop learning when practising the art of sugarcraft! They are constantly discovering exciting new ways of developing their artistic talents. The success of The Complete Book of Cake Decorating with Sugarpaste encouraged me to write this book for those of you who have mastered the basic techniques and wish to extend your skills.

In the course of my extensive travels I have been delighted to meet so many fellow enthusiasts for the art of sugarcraft, which is now flourishing all over the world. The growing use of sugarpaste, known as plastic icing in some countries, has of course enabled the ambitious decorator to create some spectacular effects more easily than with royal icing.

Beautifully decorated cakes are a memorable feature of so many celebrations, such as weddings, christenings and birthdays. Centrepieces and novelties also offer plenty of scope for showing off your expertise. Even if you are slightly daunted by such a time-consuming project as the elaborate centrepiece on page 96, I hope that it may inspire you to create a simpler scene for a special occasion.

The full-colour photographs of the finished cakes with close-ups of certain details will help you to follow the step-by-step instructions and to reproduce the different designs successfully. Patterns of all the relevant decorations are also included; many of these could be equally helpful reference material if you wish to create your own designs for cakes and special occasions.

Proportion is one of the most important aspects to consider when planning a design. Like any other artist, you should think how the different elements should be blended together to achieve the desired overall effect.

Many decorators find it difficult to choose a design that is suitable for a man's cake. The recipient's hobby can often provide an appropriate theme – I have, for example, included cakes for a golfer, an artist and a musician.

Those of you who wish to enter competitions – either as an amateur or a professional – will, I hope, enjoy the challenge of reproducing the showpieces on pages 126–131. These have been designed to demonstrate the use of different techniques, including airbrushing, at an advanced level.

May you all have as much pleasure in using this book as I have had in creating the designs.

Sylvia Coward

Part One

Cake Recipes

Here are a few of my favourite tried-and-tested cake recipes, plus a table of baking times and guidelines on the quantities of cake mixture required for the different shapes and sizes of cake shown in this book.

I have included recipes and variations for several kinds of fruit cake, including a Low-Fat Christmas Cake, and there is also a recipe for a close-textured sponge.

While fruit cake is generally used for weddings, christenings and other special occasions, it is quite acceptable to use a sponge cake if you prefer. However, sponge cake does have a couple of disadvantages which are worth bearing in mind. Firstly, the cake must be made at the last moment to ensure that it is fresh for the occasion – which obviously restricts the amount of time allowed for decoration – whereas a good fruit cake improves with age. Secondly, if a tiered effect is desired, sponge cakes require special pillars or separate stands.

FRUIT CAKE

750 g mixed dried fruit
125 g dates, stoned
125 g glacé cherries
125 g nuts, chopped
125 ml brandy
250 g butter or margarine
250 g granulated sugar
6 eggs
5 ml mixed spice
5 ml ground cinnamon
2.5 ml ground cloves
5 ml ground ginger
30 ml golden syrup
375 g plain flour
5 ml bicarbonate of soda
15 ml cold water

1 Soak the fruit and nuts overnight in the brandy.

2 Preheat the oven to 150°C.

3 Line a 225-mm square cake tin with greaseproof paper.

4 Cream the butter or margarine and sugar together in a large bowl.

5 Add the eggs, one at a time, mixing well.

6 Add the spices and the golden syrup.

7 Sift the flour into the mixture and continue mixing.

8 Add the fruit and nuts and their liquid.

9 Mix the bicarbonate of soda with the water and add to the cake mixture. The mixture should be very thick.

10 Pour the mixture into the prepared cake tin and bake for 2¼ hours.

11 Place the cake in the tin on a wire rack to cool for 30–60 minutes before turning out.

NOTES:
A Should you wish to omit the dates, increase the quantity of mixed dried fruit to 875 g.
B If desired, increase the quantity of mixed spice to 20 ml and omit the cinnamon, cloves and ginger.
C Provided the total weight of fruit is not exceeded, any chopped dried or glacé fruit may be used.
D The baked cake will be about 75 mm deep.

APPOXIMATE QUANTITIES OF FRUIT CAKE MIXTURE AND BAKING TIMES

The following quantities of fruit cake mixture and the baking times are approximate for the sizes and shapes of the relevant tins. It is advisable always to test each cake with a skewer to ensure that it is sufficiently baked.

Tin size and shape	Quantity			Baking time	
150-mm square	½	×	recipe	2	hours
175-mm square	½	×	recipe	2	hours
200-mm square	¾	×	recipe	2	hours
225-mm square	1	×	recipe	2¼	hours
250-mm square	1½	×	recipe	2¾	hours
275-mm square	2	×	recipe	3	hours
300-mm square	2½	×	recipe	3	hours
325-mm square	3	×	recipe	3½	hours
350-mm square	3½	×	recipe	3½	hours
150-mm diameter round	⅜	×	recipe	2	hours
175-mm diameter round	½	×	recipe	2	hours
200-mm diameter round	¾	×	recipe	2	hours
225-mm diameter round	¾	×	recipe	2	hours
250-mm diameter round	1	×	recipe	2¼	hours
275-mm diameter round	1½	×	recipe	2¾	hours
300-mm diameter round	2	×	recipe	3	hours
325-mm diameter round	2¼	×	recipe	3½	hours
350-mm diameter round	2¾	×	recipe	3½	hours
400-mm diameter round	4	×	recipe	4½	hours
175-mm hexagonal*	½	×	recipe	2	hours
200-mm hexagonal*	½	×	recipe	2	hours
250-mm hexagonal*	¾	×	recipe	2	hours
300-mm hexagonal*	1½	×	recipe	2¾	hours
350-mm hexagonal*	2¼	×	recipe	3½	hours
400-mm hexagonal*	3	×	recipe	3½	hours
200-mm petal (scalloped)	½	×	recipe	2	hours
250-mm petal	1	×	recipe	2¼	hours
300-mm petal	1¾	×	recipe	3	hours
350-mm petal	2½	×	recipe	3½	hours
200 × 160-mm oval	½	×	recipe	2	hours
250 × 200-mm oval	1	×	recipe	2¼	hours
300 × 250-mm oval	1½	×	recipe	2¾	hours
250 × 200-mm rectangle	1¼	×	recipe	2¾	hours
325 × 225-mm rectangle	2	×	recipe	3	hours
150 × 150-mm heart	⅜	×	recipe	2	hours
225 × 200-mm heart	¾	×	recipe	2	hours
250 × 225-mm heart	1	×	recipe	2¼	hours
300 × 265-mm heart	1½	×	recipe	2¾	hours
350 × 325-mm heart	2	×	recipe	3	hours

*NOTE: The measurements given for hexagonal tins are from point to point.

SPONGE CAKE

150 g butter or margarine
140 g granulated sugar
3 eggs
grated rind of 1 lemon
260 g plain flour
5 ml baking powder
pinch of salt
60 ml milk

1 Preheat the oven to 175°C.

2 Grease and base-line a deep 200-mm diameter cake tin.

3 Cream the butter or margarine, sugar and lemon rind.

4 Add the eggs to the creamed mixture one at a time, beating thoroughly after each egg has been added.

5 Sift the flour, baking powder and salt.

6 Gradually add the sifted dry ingredients to the creamed mixture, alternating with the milk and blending gently but thoroughly.

7 Spoon the mixture into the prepared tin and bake for 45 minutes.

8 Turn out on a wire rack and leave to cool.

LOW-FAT CHRISTMAS CAKE

300 g plain flour
10 ml baking powder
2 eggs
80 ml cooking oil
125 g soft brown sugar
60 ml milk
550 g mixed dried fruit

1 Preheat the oven to 150°C.

2 Grease and line a 175-mm square cake tin.

3 Sift the flour and baking powder together.

4 Beat the eggs.

5 Add the oil, sugar and sifted dry ingredients to the beaten eggs.

6 Add enough milk to the mixture to obtain a dropping consistency.

7 Add the mixed dried fruit and mix thoroughly.

8 Pour the mixture into the tin and bake for about 1 hour or until baked.

9 Place the cake in the tin on a wire rack to cool for 30–60 minutes before turning out.

LIGHT FRUIT CAKE

150 g prunes, stoned
150 g dried apricots
40 ml clear honey
60 ml sherry or brandy
300 g seeded raisins
150 g currants
150 g dates, pitted
175 g glacé pineapple
90 g glacé cherries
30 g mixed peel
125 g walnuts or pecans
250 g butter
225 g granulated sugar
4 eggs
275 g plain flour
5 ml baking powder
2.5 ml bicarbonate of soda
pinch of salt
5 ml ground cinnamon
2.5 ml grated nutmeg
2.5 ml allspice

1 Preheat the oven to 150°C.

2 Line a 225-mm square cake tin with double thickness of paper.

3 Steam the prunes and apricots over boiling water for 2 minutes. Remove the prune flesh and cut the apricots into halves.

4 Place the prunes and apricots in a saucepan, add the honey and sherry, bring to the boil, cover and stand.

5 Wash and dry the raisins and currants.

6 Chop the dates, pineapple, cherries, mixed peel and nuts.

7 Cream the butter and sugar. Beat in the eggs, one at a time, and continue beating until the mixture is thoroughly combined.

8 Sift the dry ingredients and the spices, mixing a little of the flour into the prepared fruit (just enough to coat).

9 Mix the dry ingredients into the creamed mixture and finally add the fruit.

10 Spoon the mixture into the prepared tin and bake for 3–3½ hours.

11 Place the cake in the tin on a wire rack to cool for 30–60 minutes before turning out.

Icing Recipes

Sugarpaste (known as plastic icing in some countries) is used for covering cakes. It is used over marzipan when covering a fruit cake and on its own on a sponge cake which must first be spread with sieved apricot jam. If desired, a generous tablespoon of liquid glucose can be added to the sugarpaste to keep it from hardening too quickly. (I do not do this, preferring to decorate the cake as close to the event as possible so the icing does not harden excessively.) A cake covered with sugarpaste is easier to cut than one coated with royal icing. Gum tragacanth can be added to sugarpaste to make a modelling paste or sugarpaste can be used on its own in certain moulds.

Royal icing is used extensively for making separate decorations or for decorating directly on to a cake covered with sugarpaste. Cakes may also be covered in royal icing (with 5 ml glycerine added to each egg white) over a marzipan base coat. Royal icing is much harder than sugarpaste.

Marzipan or almond paste is used on a fruit cake before covering with sugarpaste or royal icing. It can also be used to make moulded fruit. In this latter case it is more usual to use real marzipan which is made from ground almonds and is very much more expensive. The commercially prepared variety is generally made from apricot kernels.

Pastillage is generally used for items where strength and rigidity are needed, for example, buildings, furniture, place name markers, table napkin rings and plaques.

Butter icing (not used for any cakes in this book) is an easily prepared, soft icing and is most suitable for children's birthday cakes and for cakes served at afternoon tea.

SUGARPASTE

Makes about 1.5 kg
225 g granulated sugar
250 ml liquid glucose
125 ml water
10 ml powdered gelatine
15 ml cold water
flavouring and colouring (optional)
1 kg icing sugar, sifted
20 g white vegetable fat

1 Place the granulated sugar, glucose and water in a saucepan and heat gently to dissolve the sugar, periodically washing down the sides of the saucepan with a wet pastry brush.

2 Bring the mixture to the boil and cover the saucepan for a minute or two so that the steam can wash down the sides of the saucepan.

3 Boil to 106°C without stirring – this should take about 4 minutes.

4 Soak the gelatine in the cold water.

5 Remove the pan from the heat and, once the bubbles have subsided, add the gelatine.

6 Add flavouring and colouring (if desired) and half the icing sugar.

7 Sift the remaining icing sugar on to a large smooth work surface. Make a well in the centre of the sugar and pour the mixture into it. Add the vegetable fat, mix well, then knead the mixture until a smooth, pliable consistency is obtained.

8 Roll out and use to cover the cake while the icing is still warm.

9 Store the sugarpaste in a plastic bag in an airtight container. Do *not* keep it in the refrigerator.

NOTE: This icing can be reheated in a casserole in the oven at 110°C.

ROYAL ICING

Makes about 200 g
1 egg white
200 g icing sugar, sifted
3 drops acetic acid or 1 ml tartaric acid or 2 ml lemon juice

1 Place the egg white in a glass bowl and using a wooden spoon or mixer, beat until the egg white is frothy.

2 Add 100 g icing sugar, about 30 ml at a time, beating thoroughly after each addition.

3 Add the acetic acid, tartaric acid or lemon juice.

4 Continue adding icing sugar, about 30 ml at a time, until the consistency is like well-beaten cream and the icing will hold small peaks (about 15 minutes by hand, 5 minutes with a mixer).

5 Adjust the consistency of the icing for various types of work. For piping borders, a firmer texture is required and a softer consistency is necessary for line work.

6 To colour royal icing, use only a touch of paste colour on the end of a cocktail stick mixed into a small quantity of icing on the side of the bowl before blending with the balance.

FONDANT ICING

Makes about 1 kg
250 ml liquid glucose
1 kg icing sugar, sifted
50 ml cold water
10 ml powdered gelatine
20 g white vegetable fat
egg white (optional)

1 Remove the lid from the bottle of liquid glucose and stand the bottle in hot water to warm.

2 Set aside about 150 g of the sifted icing sugar.

3 Place the gelatine in a small container with the cold water. Place the container over hot water and leave until the gelatine has completely dissolved.

4 Melt the fat.

5 Place the remaining icing sugar in a large bowl, make a well in the centre of the sugar and add the glucose, gelatine and fat. Stir well to combine.

6 Knead the icing and adjust the consistency by either adding some of the reserved icing sugar or adding egg white until a smooth and pliable paste is formed.

7 Store the icing in a plastic bag in an airtight container. Do *not* keep it in the refrigerator.

MARZIPAN

Makes about 750 g
500 g granulated sugar
250 ml water
1 ml cream of tartar
125 g ground almonds
1 egg beaten
5 ml ratafia or almond essence

1 Dissolve the sugar in the water over a low heat. Do not allow the mixture to boil until the sugar has completely dissolved.

2 Wash down the sides of the saucepan with a wet pastry brush and allow the mixture to boil to 120°C without stirring.

3 Remove the pan from the heat and allow the mixture to cool for exactly 20 minutes.

4 Add the cream of tartar, ground almonds, egg and ratafia or almond

essence and beat the mixture with a wooden spoon until it is thick and creamy. Leave to cool.

5 Place the marzipan on a board and knead it until smooth.

6 Use immediately.

MARZIPAN

Quick and Easy Method

Makes about 1 kg
500 g ground almonds
250 g icing sugar
250 g caster sugar
10 ml brandy
8 egg yolks

1 Mix all the dry ingredients together.

2 Add the brandy and sufficient egg yolk to make a paste, taking care not to knead the mixture too much as the marzipan will become oily.

3 Use immediately.

MOULDING SUGAR

Makes about 450 g
450 g caster sugar
20 ml water

1 Place the sugar in a bowl and add the water. Mix the two ingredients together, using a fork, ensuring that there are no lumps – the sugar should be like damp sand when pressed.

2 Press the sugar into the required mould and turn out immediately on to a board. Leave to dry.

NOTE: If coloured moulding sugar is required, the colouring should be added to the water before it is mixed with the sugar so that the consistency is not affected.

MODELLING PASTE

Makes about 500 g
white margarine or vegetable fat
500 g icing sugar, sifted
25 ml gum tragacanth (purest)
15 ml cold water
15 ml powdered gelatine
15 ml boiling water
1 large egg white

1 Grease a glass mixing bowl with white margarine or vegetable fat, add the icing sugar and place the bowl over a pan of hot water to heat it.

2 Add the gum tragacanth, stirring with a wooden spoon to ensure that the mixture is heated evenly. Do not allow the sugar to become moist. Heat until the mixture is just a little warmer than blood temperature, then remove the bowl from the water.

3 Place the cold water in a container and sprinkle the gelatine on to the water. Add the boiling water and stand the container in a bowl of hot water to dissolve the gelatine. Do *not* place it on the cooker as gelatine must never get too hot.

4 Beat the egg white lightly with a fork to break it up.

5 Remove 250 g of the warm icing sugar mixture and put to one side. Add the gelatine and most of the egg white to the remaining icing sugar in the bowl. Stir, mixing quickly and well. Add the remaining icing sugar and beat thoroughly.

6 Transfer the mixture to a clean, greased bowl and, with clean hands greased with white margarine or vegetable fat, work the paste for 10–15 minutes. Add the remaining egg white if the modelling paste seems a little dry or stiff.

7 Shape the paste into a ball and grease the outside with white margarine or vegetable fat. Store the modelling paste in a plastic bag in a sealed container in the refrigerator.

8 Once or twice a week, take the paste out of the refrigerator and work it for about 5 minutes.

MODELLING PASTE

Quick and Easy Method
This paste improves with age. It should always be stored in an airtight container.

Makes about 500 g
500 g sugarpaste
15 ml gum tragacanth

1 Mix the sugarpaste and gum tragacanth together and knead thoroughly.

2 Store the modelling paste in a plastic bag in an airtight container. Do *not* keep it in the refrigerator.

3 Allow the paste to mature for at least a week before use.

4 Knead the paste thoroughly before use. If the paste is a bit dry and crumbly, break small pieces off, dip them into water and then knead them thoroughly.

NOTE: Sprinkle some cornflour on the work surface, if necessary, when working with light colours or use vegetable fat if you are working with dark colours.

PASTILLAGE

Makes about 250 g
250 g royal icing
5 ml gum tragacanth
dry, sifted icing sugar
cornflour

1 Mix the royal icing and gum tragacanth together.

2 Add icing sugar gradually to obtain a pliable dough that is no longer sticky.

3 Lightly dust a piece of glass or board lightly with cornflour, roll out the pastillage and cut out the desired shapes. If the pastillage is too dry, break off a piece, dip it into water and knead it thoroughly.

4 Turn the cut-out shapes every few hours until they are thoroughly dry.

NOTE: Pastillage is best used immediately, but it can be stored in a plastic bag in an airtight container for a few days.

GUM ARABIC GLAZE

gum Arabic
hot water

1 Mix the gum Arabic with hot water to obtain a painting consistency.

2 Paint completed, moulded flowers and leaves to create a porcelain effect.

EDIBLE GLITTER

50 ml hot water
25 g gum Arabic

1 Preheat the oven to 140°C.

2 Pour the hot water into a bowl and sprinkle the gum Arabic over the water. Stand the bowl in hot water, stirring gently to dissolve the gum.

3 Strain the mixture through a piece of nylon.

4 Brush the mixture on to a clean baking tray or glass surface and place in the oven until dry.

5 Brush or scrape the dry glitter off the tray and crush it to obtain fine flakes.

6 Store the glitter in an airtight jar.

NOTE: Glitter may be coloured by adding the colouring to the water when mixing.

Glossary of Tools, Special Ingredients and Equipment

Certain basic tools, pieces of equipment and special ingredients are essential when executing the various cake decorating techniques. However, there are numerous additional items you may want to add to your collection of equipment in order to create a variety of different effects. The equipment listed here is by no means all that is available, but most of the items used for the cake designs featured in this book are included.

Although it is obviously an advantage to have all the appropriate tools and pieces of equipment available, you may not always have access to them. With a little ingenuity, you will find items around the house which can be substituted most successfully.

Anger tool: A multi-purpose wooden tool which is most commonly used for hollowing-out small flowers, although it has many other uses.

Ball tools: Available in a variety of sizes, these are used for modelling and moulding flowers and figures.

Brushes: It is essential to build up a collection of good quality artist's paintbrushes in a selection of sizes, for creating special effects.

Crimpers: Available in an assortment of designs, these are used to create a variety of patterns on cakes by 'pinching' the sugarpaste. Two of the most attractive and easy-to-use crimpers are the V-shape and the scallop.

Florist's wire and fuse wire: Cut into short lengths, either type of wire may be inserted into moulded flowers to facilitate the making-up of sprays, which are then attached to the cake

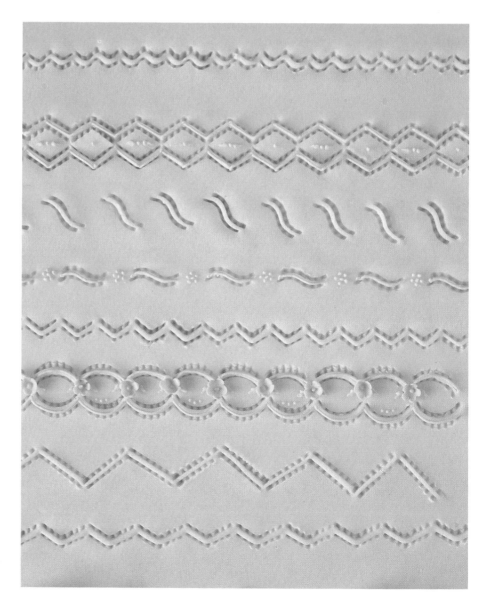

Some of the patterns that can be created by using different crimpers

with royal icing. The wire stems should *never* be inserted directly into the cake.

Florist's tape: Available in white, brown, light and dark green, this is used for taping the wires of moulded flowers.

Flower cutters: Available in a variety of shapes and sizes, these metal or plastic cutters are used to make many different kinds of flowers.

Flower formers: The various plastic and wooden shapes used to make moulded flowers.

Flower nails: These are usually flat metal or plastic discs on spikes but a range of different nails is available. They are used for piped royal icing flowers.

Flower or leaf veiners: Rubber or plastic shapes that are pressed on to modelling paste to create the effect of the veining on flowers and leaves.

Frill rulers: Available in a variety of lengths, these scalloped cutters create a frilled or scalloped edge when used to cut out modelling paste or pastillage.

Frisket: Available from art shops, this is a useful masking material.

Gum Arabic: A glaze, used to create a porcelain effect on sugar flowers, this can also be used to make Edible Glitter (page 15).

Gum tragacanth: Available from specialist cake decorating shops and pharmacies, this powder gives elasticity and acts as a drying agent. It is an essential ingredient in the modelling paste used to make moulded flowers.

Hobby or icing knife: A small knife which is required for certain types of designs in order to cut out the modelling paste or pastillage properly.

COLOURINGS

The choice of colourings currently available to the cake decorator is very wide. There are pastes, liquids, powders that are mixed with a few drops of water or even alcohol, and powders that are brushed on after mixing with a little cornflour to create a pale shading.

● Paste colours are most suitable for all types of icing because they do not significantly alter the consistency of the icing. Unfortunately, it is necessary to use a considerable amount of this type of colouring to achieve dark colours and then not always successfully.

● Liquid colours blend in very easily but to obtain dark colours it is again necessary to add a lot, which can soften your icing too much. It will then be necessary to add more icing sugar or a little cornflour to sugarpaste. Of course, liquid colouring is used for an airbrush. Ideally those colourings specially designated for use with an airbrush are the most suitable – only a few drops are needed mixed with about 5 ml of water. The colouring should not have any granules in it.

● Powder colours which are water-soluble are best mixed to a paste with a few drops of water before they are added to icing. Because the water dissolves the colour granules, this also prevents streaks of colour in the icing. The advantage of these colours is generally evident in the dark colours, such as red, black and brown.

● Powder colours which are used for blushing, brushing or dusting are first mixed with cornflour. These are used dry on flowers or figures.

● Gold and silver powders are not, technically-speaking, food colourings but are used generally in minute quantities in the confectionery trade to add details to royal icing or modelling paste. Used so sparingly, these powders are not considered to be harmful. The powders are mixed with caramel oil flavouring or alcohol to obtain a consistency suitable for painting.

Hints on mixing colours

If you cannot buy the exact shade of colouring you require, try mixing your own colours. Here are some suggestions:

Golden-yellow	*lemon yellow plus a touch of orange or red*
Orange	*lemon yellow plus red*
Tan	*brown plus white and a little yellow*
Grey	*black plus white*
Lime green	*green plus some yellow*
Sea green	*green plus royal blue*
Turquoise	*blue plus green*
Flesh	*pink plus a little yellow*
Salmon pink	*pink plus orange*
Magenta	*red and blue*
Brick red	*brown plus red*
Maroon	*red and blue, plus a touch of brown*

How to shade modelling paste

1   Colour 50 g of modelling paste (page 14) to the darkest shade you require.

2   To 25 g of the coloured modelling paste add 25 g white modelling paste to form a second shade.

3   To 25 g of the second shade, add 25 g white modelling paste to create a third shade.

Icing bags: An alternative to paper cones for use in piping, the nylon or plastic icing bag is preferable to the rigid, syringe-type.

Lifters: Made from two pieces of thin board, each about 380 × 250 mm, these are used to lift the marzipan or sugarpaste on to the cake.

Moulds: Commercially available in a wide variety of designs, including animals and figures, these are generally made of plastic and may be filled with caster sugar, chocolate or modelling paste.

Nozzles: See **Tubes.**

Painting knife: Available from art shops, this is used to facilitate the lifting of petals, leaves and so on.

Palette: For mixing colourings for cake decorating, a small plastic artist's palette is extremely useful.

Paper cones: Individually made from greaseproof paper, these are generally favoured by cake decorators for use with icing tubes. The cones can be made large or small to suit the particular purpose.

Ribbon inserter: The flat end of this double-ended tool is used to make slits in icing to allow for the insertion of ribbon: the other end is sometimes pointed, to create a *broderie anglaise* effect, or maybe a ridged cone for use in moulding flowers.

Roller: Made of chrome or plastic, this is necessary when rolling out modelling paste for moulded flowers and similar items.

Rolling board: A solid wooden board with a smooth covering, preferably melamine, this is essential when rolling out modelling paste or pastillage.

Rolling pin: A good quality rolling pin is vital when rolling out sugarpaste or marzipan. A ribbed rolling pin can be used to create interesting effects on plaques and other surfaces.

Scissors: Essential for fine, detailed work, sharp embroidery scissors are the best choice.

Shears or wire cutters: These are used for cutting florist's wire or fuse wire when making up sprays of flowers.

Smoothers: Available in pairs, made of plastic and rectangular in shape, these are used for smoothing the sides and top edges of marzipan and sugarpaste covering a cake.

Stamens: Commercially produced, these are available in a variety of lengths and designs to suit the many different kinds of flowers.

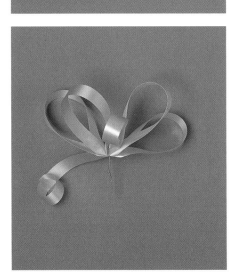
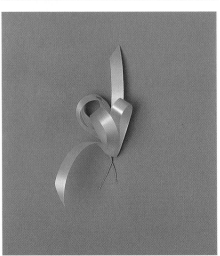

About 500 mm of florist's ribbon are needed to make a decorative bow, following the steps shown in the photographs

Tape cutter: This is used for cutting florist's tape into four, lengthways, making it possible to tape very fine wires smoothly.

Tube cleaning brush: Rather like a miniature bottle brush in appearance, this cleans tubes easily and thoroughly after use.

Tubes: Also referred to as nozzles, icing tubes are available in a wide variety of shapes and sizes under several brandnames. Types of tubes available include writing tubes, star tubes, petal tubes, drop flower tubes and leaf tubes. Unfortunately, there is no international uniformity in the way in which they are numbered by the manufacturers, except perhaps for some of the writing tubes, and it is therefore a good idea to select the best tubes from each brand according to your purpose.

Veining and fluting tools: The curved ends of these tools are extremely useful when moulding flowers or figures.

Workbox: To store all your tools and equipment neatly and safely, invest in a solid, sectioned workbox.

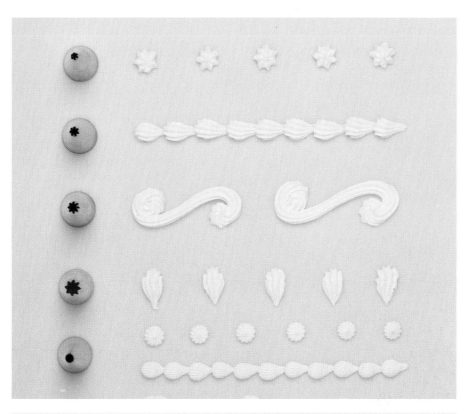

Some examples of piping with star, petal and drop flower tubes

Glossary of Decorating Techniques

Advanced cake decorators will already be familiar with the basic techniques. This section is intended to serve primarily as a reference to the different techniques used to decorate the cakes illustrated in this book.

AIRBRUSHING

An airbrush is primarily an artist's precision instrument, but some models are sold specifically for cake decorating. Unfortunately, airbrushes are expensive. Brushing with dusting powder is an alternative way of achieving similar effects.

An airbrush is a metal pen-like instrument connected by a hose to a compressor. (Models with separate compressed air cannisters are not as successful.) Generally it has a small metal cup, close to the tip or nozzle. This holds the relevant liquid food colouring mixed with about 5 ml water. Only use liquid food colourings having the same consistency as water. Do *not* use paste or concentrated liquid or powder colours as these often contain pigments or fibres which do not dissolve completely. The particles may clog your airbrush and cause splattering.

A small trigger or lever is depressed to regulate the volume of colour which is sprayed from the airbrush. Where an airbrush has been used to decorate cakes illustrated (see Blue for a Boy, page 62, for example) in this book, the effects have been created by holding the airbrush about 250 mm away from the surface.

Designs or pictures can be created on a cake by using a stencil, cut from plastic or acetate masking film (obtainable from art shops), thin cardboard or stiff paper with a craft knife, to allow for colour to be sprayed on certain sections and others to be blocked out. A paper or plastic doily also makes a good stencil. Make sure that the stencil or doily remains perfectly flat when spraying. Moulded white leaves or flowers may be sprayed with an airbrush very successfully.

How to use an airbrush

1 Cover the work surface with newspaper or absorbent kitchen paper before you start.
2 Place a bowl of hot water beside you.
3 Plug in the compressor and connect the airbrush following the manufacturer's instructions.
4 Fill the colour cup with about 5 ml water and then add a few drops of the desired colour.
5 Hold the airbrush lightly in your hand, as you would a pen or pencil.
6 Switch on the compressor.
7 Practise spraying on to the newspaper or absorbent kitchen paper by depressing the main lever or trigger until the colour emerges.
8 The further away you are from the surface to be decorated, the wider and finer the spray. The closer you are, the narrower the spray, so a line is formed.
9 When changing colours during spraying, flush the airbrush with water by placing the tip or nozzle of the airbrush in a bowl of hot water and holding the main lever back fully. Continue this flushing until all traces of colour are washed away. Repeat this procedure before putting the airbrush away.

NOTE: The needle and tip or nozzle of the airbrush are very delicate so take extreme care not to damage them in any way.

The wide range of icing tubes enables the cake decorator to achieve extremely varied results. Writing tubes are used for embroidery and figure piping as well as for inscriptions, dots and lines. Star tubes are used for making shells, stars, scrolls and similar items. Petal tubes are used for piping a variety of flowers.

Drop flower tubes enable you to make a whole flower with one pressing of the paper cone. Ribbon tubes – available with either one or both edges serrated – are used for piping ribbons or bands and for basket weave. Leaf tubes are also available, as well as a number of other tubes designed to create special effects.

Basket weave: Pipe a vertical line of the required length in royal icing with a ribbon tube, then pipe a number of short lines across it, leaving a space the width of the tube between them. Pipe another vertical line, just covering the ends of the short ones. Pipe short lines over this vertical line to give the effect of weaving. Repeat as necessary.

Crimping: A variety of patterns can be created by using the different crimpers that are available. To be effective, the edge of the cake should be measured to ensure that the chosen pattern will fit perfectly. Dip the ends of the crimper in cornflour to prevent them sticking to the freshly applied sugarpaste.

Embroidery: Floral and other designs can be piped with a fine writing tube and royal icing of soft peak consistency on to a cake either free-hand or by first marking the outlines with a pin. Alternatively, use a glass stencil. For brush embroidery, hold a 2-mm wide flat brush at an angle of 45° and brush the icing from the outer edge inwards, spreading it more thinly towards the centre. Work a small section at a time to prevent the icing drying. For eyelet embroidery, cut out the design in a frill, or other item made from modelling paste, with eyelet embroidery cutters. Pipe dots and scrolls around each opening with a No. 1 tube and royal icing to complete the design. For a picot edge, use a No. 0 or 1 writing tube and royal icing to pipe a row of small dots. Pipe three dots under the spaces between the first four dots, then two dots underneath and finally one, forming a triangular shape. Miss one dot in the original row and repeat the pattern as necessary.

Basket weave and crimping, Horn of Plenty, page 68

Above: brush embroidery, Mothering Sunday, page 116; below: eyelet embroidery, His and Hers, page 48

Filigree and lace pieces: Use a fine writing tube and royal icing to pipe on to waxed paper taped over the required pattern. Wipe the end of the tube with a damp cloth after piping each piece to ensure clean lines. Leave the pieces to dry for at least 2 hours before attaching them to the cake with dots of royal icing. Filigree and lace pieces are very fragile and it is therefore advisable to make more than are actually needed.

Floodwork: Sometimes called run-in work, this is the technique of filling in a design (for example, a collar) with royal icing thinned to the right consistency with a few drops of water. Tape the design on to a piece of glass and then tape a piece of waxed paper on top of the design.

Outline the design using a fine writing tube and royal icing of firm peak consistency. Using a paper cone filled with thinned royal icing, fill in the design, starting close to the outline at the furthest point from you. When the area is almost full, use a small paintbrush to push the icing to the outline.

It is always advisable to make a duplicate of any floodwork item to ensure that it is thoroughly dry if needed as a replacement.

Glass stencil: Trace the required design on a piece of paper, then carefully outline the design on the back of the paper with a pencil. Cover with a piece of glass (the design will therefore be reversed), securing with tape. Pipe directly on to the glass, using a fine writing tube and royal icing. When the icing is hard, press the design against freshly applied sugarpaste and lift the glass off.

Ribbon insertion: Especially when used in conjunction with embroidery, ribbon insertion is a most effective decoration on the side of a cake. It is important to mark the positions for the slots accurately with a pin before cutting the sugarpaste with a ribbon inserter (or craft knife).

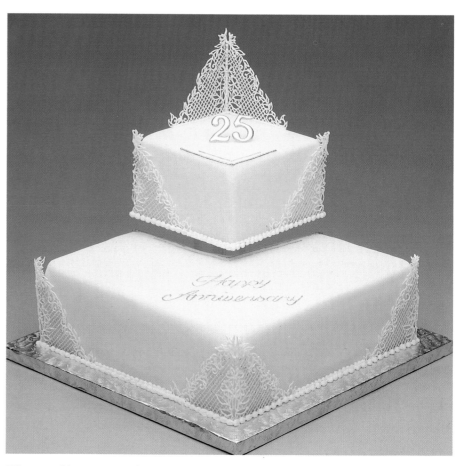

Filigree and lace pieces, Silver Celebration, page 56

Ribbon insertion, Twin Blessings, page 64

Roping: Using a small or medium star tube and royal icing, hold the paper cone at an angle of 45° and maintain a constant pressure as you pipe a 'comma' curving downwards, then to the left, finally flicking slightly to the right. Repeat as necessary.

Sugar moulding: Mix 500 g caster sugar and 20 ml water together thoroughly with a fork to ensure that there are no lumps. Spoon the mixture into a mould, press down well and turn out, tapping gently on the top if necessary to release the sugar. Leave to dry. A few drops of food colouring may be added to the water before mixing, if wished.

Sugar moulding, Sugar Hearts, page 124

USING MOULDS

One of the simpler ways of making cake decorations is to use moulds for shaping modelling paste (page 14). However, with a little imagination and artistic trimming, very attractive decorations can be created.

To make hollow shapes, for example an open shell or an egg:
1   Roll out some modelling paste to about 3 mm thick.
2   Rub a little cornflour on to the reverse side of the modelling paste and press into the mould firmly, thus ensuring that any markings will be transferred to the paste.
3   Using a craft knife, trim away any excess modelling paste.
4   Leave the modelling paste to set in the mould, but move the paste occasionally to ensure it has not stuck to the mould.

To make solid shapes:
1   Thoroughly knead some modelling paste and roll it into a ball so that the paste is smooth and there are no cracks.
2   If necessary, depending on the shape of the mould, roll the paste into a sausage.
3   Rub a little cornflour on the outside of the modelling paste before pressing it firmly into the mould.
4   Using a craft knife, trim away any excess modelling paste from the back of the mould so that the shape lies flat when turned out.
5   Immediately turn the shape out on to a work surface thickly dusted with cornflour and leave to dry. Move frequently to prevent sticking.

NOTES: As cornflour marks can show on dark colours, you may paint over the dry moulded item with water. This will also give it a glossy finish. Do not put cornflour into the mould as you will lose detail.

Lavender Lady, page 70

Moulded Decorations

These beautiful and realistic flowers and leaves are moulded from modelling paste. The flowers included in this section are all featured on cakes in this book. With a little ingenuity and practice, you can of course create many other varieties, following the techniques shown here. Use books and photographs for reference or, for the very best results, lovely fresh flowers.

Modelling paste is also used to make the acorn, pine cones, baby's face and butterfly shown on pages 31 and 32.

AZALEA

EQUIPMENT
stamens
florist's tape
26-g florist's wire
tinned copper fuse wire
white modelling paste (page 14)
petal cutters or pattern (page 172)
hibiscus petal veiner
anger tool
pink dusting powder
wooden or plastic flower stand
pieces of sponge or cotton wool
maroon food colouring
5/0 paintbrush

1 Cut ten stamens to a length of 30 mm and one to a length of 40 mm.

2 Secure the stamens to a length of taped 26-g wire using a piece of fuse wire.

3 Tape over the wire with florist's tape to neaten.

4 Roll out the modelling paste and cut out one piece using a three-petal cutter or the pattern, then cut out two single petals.

5 Press each petal against the hibiscus petal veiner.

6 Using the anger tool, frill the outer, shaped edges of the petals.

7 Using dusting powder, shade the inside of the petals pink to within a few millimetres of the edge.

8 Gently crease the centre petal of the three-petal piece.

9 Moisten the base of the three-petal piece and then attach it to the wired stamens, pressing firmly to secure.

10 Attach the two single petals to each other with water and then to the three-petal piece.

11 Set the azalea on a flower stand, supporting it with sponge or cotton wool as necessary and leave to dry thoroughly.

12 Using maroon food colouring, paint dots in the centre of the three-petal piece and part of the petals on either side.

NOTE: The calyx is a small five-pointed star shape. It is not necessary to add a calyx to the flower unless, of course, you are making specimen flowers for a show, in which case it is essential to work from a real flower.

CARNATION

EQUIPMENT
modelling paste (page 14)
pattern (page 173)
icing knife, hobby knife or small
    scissors
anger tool
water
covered florist's wire
green florist's tape
paintbrush
food colourings
white stamens

1 To make a small flower, roll out the modelling paste thinly and using the pattern, cut out a scalloped round about 50 mm in diameter. Using an icing knife, cut tiny 1-mm slits into the paste all round the edge.

2 Frill the edge of the circle with an anger tool. Paint a cross on the modelling paste with water and pinch the centre of the circle from underneath to form a point, making sure that the edges do not stick to one another. Open up the flower with the anger tool to give it a 'fluffy' appearance.

3 Push the looped end of a piece of 26-g covered florist's wire through the flower and allow it to dry. When dry,

you may tape a piece of green florist's tape around the base.

4 To make a large flower, repeat Steps 1 and 2 above three or four times and then join the parts with water, pressing them together to form a large carnation. (Touch the edges of the petals with a paintbrush dipped in red or pink food colouring, if desired.)

5 Roll a ball of green modelling paste about half the size of a marble and hollow out the centre into a cup shape. Thin the edge with your fingers and then cut it into five equal sections. Cut each section into a pointed shape.

6 Thread a piece of covered florist's wire, with a closed hook at one end, through the calyx and then stick a small ball of green paste on top of the wire inside the calyx to secure it. Paint the inside of the calyx with water. Attach the calyx to the flower by inserting the flower into the hollowed calyx.

7 Cut three lengths of white stamen 'stalk' and curl one end of each by scraping the blade of a pair of scissors or the back of a knife along it. Dip the straight ends of the stamens into water and then insert them into the centre of the carnation.

NOTE: When requiring a long-stemmed carnation, tape an extra length of wire to the stem. Cut pieces of florist's tape into leaf shapes and twist them on to the stem where required.

CYMBIDIUM ORCHID

EQUIPMENT
modelling paste (page 14)
curved modelling tool
dusting powder
paintbrush
food colourings
anger tool
flower cutter or pattern (page 173)
ball tool
orchid former
water
leaf veiner
hollow mould

1 Roll a small piece of white modelling paste, about twice the size of a large pea, into a cylinder about 15 mm long with rounded ends. Using a curved modelling tool, or the back of a paintbrush, press a hollow into its length and then curve the cylinder slightly. Brush with dusting powder to match the shade of the petals. Paint tiny dots of food colouring on the inside curve and set aside to dry.

2 Roll out some modelling paste in the colour of your choice to form the trumpet or lip of the orchid. Leave the paste slightly thicker where the rounded part of the lip will be when it is cut. Using the patterns, cut out the trumpet and flute along the centre curved portion using an anger tool, then hollow the side sections slightly with a ball tool. Place the trumpet or lip on an orchid former to dry in the required shape, pulling the centre section downwards. Colour the trumpet or lip with dusting powder if desired.

Carnations and cymbidium orchids, It's Our Day, page 58

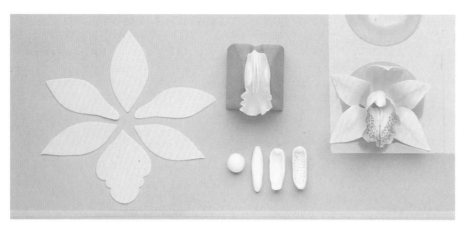

3 With yellow modelling paste, roll two very thin cylinders about 2 mm thick and 10 mm long, each one tapering to a point. Attach the cylinders to the trumpet or lip with a little water.

4 Cut out five petals from the same colour modelling paste used for the trumpet, using a flower cutter or the pattern. Use a leaf veiner to mark the petals with fine lines. Run a ball tool along the edges of each one to refine them. Colour the petals with dusting powder if wished, then place the petals over a curved shape.

5 Grease a hollow mould and add a ball of paste the size of a large pea. Flatten it, paint it with water and then attach the petals and trumpet to create an orchid as shown.

DAISIES

EQUIPMENT
modelling paste (page 14)
food colourings
daisy cutter or pattern (page 172)
large pin
flower stand
small piece of tulle
taped fuse wire
leaf cutter
fresh leaf or leaf veiner

1 Roll out some modelling paste in the colour of your choice and cut out the daisies, using a daisy cutter or the pattern.

2 Use the large pin to mark the lines on each petal, as shown. Attach two daisies to each other with water and place on a flower stand to set.

3 Roll a small ball of yellow model-ling paste and press it against a piece of tulle to mark.

4 Attach the marked, flattened balls to the centre of each daisy with a little water and set aside to dry.

5 For the stems, use a piece of taped fuse wire. Bend the end of the wire and dip it into water. Roll a ball of green modelling paste and mould it to a cone shape, then flatten the top and thread the wire through. Leave to dry.

6 Attach the daisies to the stems with a little water or royal icing.

7 Roll out some pale green modelling paste and cut out the leaves, using a leaf cutter.

8 Vein the leaves, using a fresh leaf or a rubber veiner.

9 Moisten the back of the leaves, attach fuse wire stems. Shape to give a natural appearance and leave to dry.

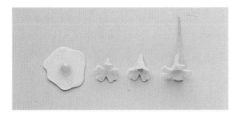

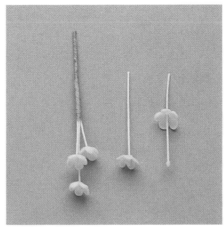

IVY LEAVES

EQUIPMENT
pale avocado green modelling paste
(page 14)
ivy leaf cutters or pattern (page 173)
violet leaf veiner
75-mm lengths of covered fuse wire
dimpled sponge
dark green dusting powder
5 ml gum Arabic dissolved in 15 ml
boiling water

1 Roll out the avocado green model-ling paste and, using an ivy leaf cutter or the pattern, cut out the leaves, leaving the paste slightly thicker at the base.

2 Press the leaves against a violet leaf veiner.

3 Dip one end of the lengths of covered fuse wire in water and insert them in the bases of the leaves.

4 Gently shape the leaves and leave them on dimpled sponge to dry.

5 Shade the leaves, using dark green dusting powder.

6 Finally, glaze the leaves by painting with the gum Arabic solution.

NOTE: For a variegated leaf, break off small pieces of white modelling paste and roll them on to the green paste before cutting out.

FILLER FLOWERS

All bell-shaped flowers such as daphne, hyacinth and primula are made in the same way, although the number of petals will vary.

EQUIPMENT
modelling paste (page 14)
paintbrush
flower cutter or small scissors
anger tool
large pin
taped fuse wire
stamens (optional)

1 Roll a piece of modelling paste into a ball the size of a pea. Shape it into a 'hat' shape with your fingers, then place the wide part on a board and thin the paste by rolling outwards, using the handle of a paintbrush.

2 Place an appropriate flower cutter over the long centre section, or use small scissors, and cut out the desired shape. Turn the flower over and hollow the inside with an anger tool.

3 If required, mark each petal with a pin by making a line along its length.

4 Bend the end of a piece of taped fuse wire, dip it in water and thread it through the flower, thus enabling you to wire small flowers together in sprays. Stamens may be added, if wished.

FORGET-ME-NOTS

EQUIPMENT
modelling paste (page 14)
flower cutter or pattern (page 173)
ball tool
stamens or thin taped fuse wire
water

1 Roll out some modelling paste and cut out the flowers using a flower cutter or the pattern. (Use either pink or blue modelling paste.)

2 Hollow each flower slightly with a ball tool.

3 Dip the stamens, or lengths of thin taped fuse wire, into water and insert one into the centre of each flower.

MIMOSA

EQUIPMENT
taped fuse wire
yellow modelling paste (page 14)
small container of water
absorbent kitchen paper
granulated sugar

1 Bend over one end of the taped wire.

2 Roll a tiny ball of modelling paste. Dip the bent end of the wire in water and then insert the wire in the modelling paste ball. Neaten and set aside to dry.

3 Dip the little modelling paste ball on wire in water, gently dab it on the absorbent kitchen paper and then dip it in the sugar. Leave to dry.

MOCK ORANGE BLOSSOM

EQUIPMENT
white sewing cotton
tinned copper fuse wire
yellow and green liquid food
   colourings
white and green modelling paste
   (page 14)
florist's tape
small daphne cutter
petal cutter or pattern (page 172)

1 Roll the white cotton loosely around your forefinger to a thickness of about 2 mm.

2 Cut a length of fuse wire and slip it through the looped cotton to secure. Twist the wire tightly to hold the cotton firmly. Cut through the cotton on one side.

3 Dip the ends of the cut cotton into yellow food colouring and set aside.

4 Mix together some white and green modelling paste to make a very, very pale green. Roll a miniature sausage of this paste to form the pistil of the flower. Moisten the end of a piece of fuse wire, insert it into the sausage and leave to dry.

5 Tape the pistil and stamens together with florist's tape.

6 Using a small daphne cutter, make a green calyx by following the steps for filler flowers (page 27). Insert the wire with stamens and pistil, moisten with water in order to attach and leave to dry.

7 Roll out some white modelling paste and, using a petal cutter or the pattern, cut out four petals. Frill the round edges very slightly and then hollow the petals.

8 Moisten the inside of the calyx with water, attach the petals and leave to dry.

Mock orange blossom, Hearts and Flowers, page 46

NARCISSUS

EQUIPMENT
taped fuse wire
modelling paste (page 14)
narcissus cutters or pattern (page 173)
small ball tool
large pin
yellow royal icing (page 13)
tube: No. 1

1 Bend over one end of the taped wire and then bend again sideways.

2 Roll a ball of modelling paste for the centre cup, hollow and cut as for filler flowers (page 27), using either narcissus cutters or the pattern and a small ball tool.

3 Moisten the bent end of wire, thread it through the hollowed cup and set aside to dry.

4 Roll out some modelling paste and cut out the second part of flower.

5 Using a large pin, mark a line down the centre of each petal.

6 Moisten the centre and insert the wire with the bell-shaped cup. Set aside to dry.

7 With a No. 1 tube and yellow royal icing, pipe a centre into the bell of the flower by pressing down firmly and then pulling away gently to form the pistil.

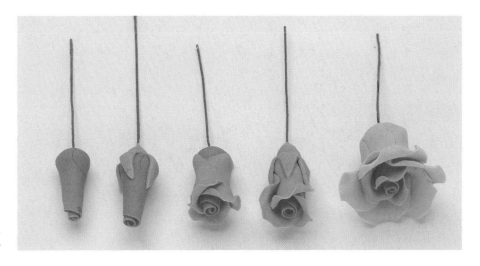

ROSE AND BUD

EQUIPMENT
florist's tape
florist's wire
pale pink, pale and dark green
  modelling paste (page 14)
water
patterns for calyx and rose petals
  (page 172)
painting knife
ball tool
small scissors

1 Cut green florist's tape into four, lengthways, cover a piece of florist's wire and bend over one end. Roll pale pink modelling paste into a ball the size of a large pea. Roll into a sausage-shape and then flatten along the length of the roll, flattening one side only.

2 Dip the curved end of the covered florist's wire into water and place it on one end of the flattened modelling paste. Roll the modelling paste around itself to make a centre for the rose. Set aside to dry.

3 Add the calyx at this stage to form a rosebud. (If a half rose is desired, continue from Step 9 for instructions on how to mould the petals). Roll out some of each shade of green modelling paste separately, then place one on top of the other, attaching the two layers with water if necessary.

4 Roll out the two layers together and cut out the calyx using a calyx cutter or the pattern. Gently lift the calyx with a painting knife and place it, dark side up, on the palm of your hand.

5 Move the small end of a ball tool along the length of each sepal and then hollow out the centre of the calyx. Pinch the ends of each sepal to make a point. Using small scissors, cut a tiny strip away from the base of each sepal.

6 Turn the calyx over and paint water on its centre and a little way along each sepal.

7 Join the calyx to the rose by pushing the wire stem through the centre of the calyx, the light side touching the rose.

SWEET PEA

EQUIPMENT
pale pink or lilac and green modelling
  paste (page 14)
taped fuse wire
cutters or patterns for petals and
  leaves (page 172)
ball tool
pink or violet dusting powder
small star cutter
pointed modelling tool
dimpled sponge
paintbrush

1 Shape the pink or lilac modelling paste to form the centre of the sweet pea, as shown.

2 Bend over the end of a length of taped fuse wire, moisten with water and insert it in the centre of the sweet pea. Set aside to dry. When dry, bend the wire close to the centre.

3 Roll out the pink and lilac modelling paste and, using the pattern, cut out the petals. Press a centre fold into each petal and flute the rounded edges with a ball tool.

4 Moisten the base of each petal with water and attach to the centre of the sweet pea. Pull the back petal out slightly and allow the flower to dry thoroughly. Brush with pink or violet dusting powder.

8 Roll a piece of dark green paste into a ball the size of a small pea. Flatten one side slightly, paint the flattened side with water and push the wire stem through the ball, flat side uppermost, to form the hip of the rose.

9 Roll out pink modelling paste and cut out three smaller rose petals with a petal cutter or use the pattern. Place a petal in the palm of your hand and hollow and flute it with a ball tool.

10 Paint the base of each petal with water and attach each to the cone, curving the edges outward. Set aside to dry. Following Steps 3–8 above, add the calyx at this stage to form a half rose.

11 For a fuller rose, cut out five larger petals and hollow and flute the petals with a ball tool in the palm of your hand. Paint with water and attach to the cone with the three petals attached. Add the calyx, if desired, following Steps 3–8 above, and gently curve back the sepals of the calyx.

Step-by-step photographs showing how to make miniature roses using modelling paste. Crescent sprays of these flowers are used to decorate Ballet Shoes, page 76

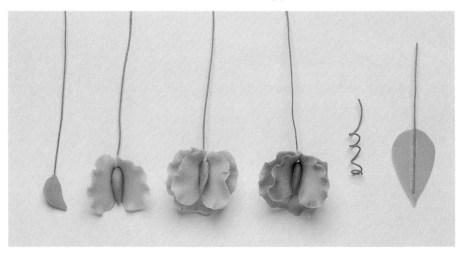

5 If wished, make a calyx following the steps for filler flowers (page 27) and using a small star cutter. Attach the calyx to the sweet pea after moistening it with water.

6 Cut out the leaves, using the pattern, and vein them with a modelling tool. Leave to dry on dimpled sponge.

7 Form the sweet pea tendrils by winding taped wire around the handle of a paintbrush.

ACORN

EQUIPMENT
light brown and light green modelling paste (page 14)
taped fuse wire or 26-g florist's wire
brown stamens
large ball tool
modelling tool

1 Roll a piece of light brown modelling paste into a ball, about the size of a large marble, then roll gently between the palms of the hands to form an oval shape.

2 Cut 10 mm off the top of a stamen and push this 10-mm piece into one end of the oval shape. Loop the end of a piece of taped wire and insert it in the other end of the oval shape. Set aside to dry.

3 Mix light brown and light green modelling paste together, to create a mottled effect.

4 Roll a ball of this paste and, using the large ball tool, hollow it out to form a cup.

5 Insert the wire and the oval shape into the cup, moistening slightly with water, then press the end of the modelling tool against the outside of cup to make a number of marks. Press the cup against the oval to attach firmly. Leave to dry.

NOTE: A pattern for the oak leaves, also used to decorate Fifty Years Young, is given on page 78.

PINE CONES

EQUIPMENT
brown modelling paste (page 14)
small scissors
taped fuse wire (optional)

1 Roll a large marble-sized ball of brown modelling paste into an egg shape.

2 Starting from the base and moving up to the point, use small scissors to snip small sections from the modelling paste. Ensure that the cut sections are not in straight lines but are positioned in alternate spaces.

3 If desired, a wire stem can be added.

BABY'S OR CHILD'S FACE

EQUIPMENT

flesh-coloured modelling paste
  (page 14)
cornflour
mould for baby's face
cocktail stick
dusting brush
pink dusting powder
5/0 paintbrush
white food colouring (Clem's powder)
brown and pink liquid food colourings

1 Knead some flesh-coloured modelling paste thoroughly and then roll it into a ball.

2 Place a little cornflour on the palm of your hand and roll the ball of modelling paste in the cornflour. Using your thumb, firmly press the modelling paste into the mould and gently shape the paste to form the back of the head. The back of the head can be left rough and piped over with royal icing to resemble hair, if necessary.

3 Break a cocktail stick in half, dip the broken end in water and insert it in the neck. Set aside to dry.

4 Brush the cheeks with pink dusting powder mixed with a little cornflour.

5 Paint the eyes with white colouring.

6 Paint the lips with a little brown and pink colouring mixed together.

7 Paint the brown in the eyes and eyebrows.

8 Paint the hair.

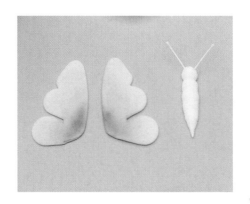

BUTTERFLY

EQUIPMENT

modelling paste (page 14)
butterfly wing cutter or pattern
  (page 173)
dusting powder
cornflour
5/0 paintbrush
tube: No. 2 or 3
royal icing (page 13)
waxed paper
sponge or cotton wool
20-mm long stamens

1 Roll out some modelling paste.

2 Cut out two wings, one left and one right, using the cutter or pattern. Leave them to dry on a level surface, turning frequently.

3 Colour the wings with the desired shade of dusting powder mixed with cornflour.

4 With a No. 2 or 3 tube and royal icing, pipe the head and body on to waxed paper. Immediately, press the wings into the body and support with sponge or cotton wool.

5 Insert two stamens as feelers and leave the wings to dry thoroughly.

Table Napkin Ring, page 121

Piped Decorations

Piped flowers are great fun to make and are pretty, delicate decorations on plaques, ornaments and novelties. Although, in recent years, cake decorators have rather deserted piped flowers for the moulded varieties, it is well worth making the effort to become skilful in piping these little blossoms. They make a charming addition to cakes for all occasions and are especially popular as a decoration for Easter eggs.

APPLE BLOSSOM FLOWER, BUD AND LEAF

EQUIPMENT
tubes: medium petal, small writing and leaf
white, pink and green royal icing (page 13)
40-mm square waxed paper flower nail

1 Fill a medium petal tube with pink and white royal icing, placing the pink icing on the side of the paper cone to line up with the wider opening of the petal tube and then adding the white icing. Fill a small writing tube (or a plain cone cut to size) with green icing. Fix a small square of waxed paper to the top of the flower nail with a touch of icing.

2 To make a blossom, hold the flower nail in your left hand (right, if left-handed). In the other hand, hold the tube of pink and white icing at an angle of about 30° to the surface of the nail, with the wider opening (where the pink icing is) to the centre of the nail. The narrow opening in the tube must be slightly raised from the nail.

3 Press the paper cone, moving the tube very slightly towards the outer edge of the nail and, at the same time, turning the nail very slightly in an anti-clockwise direction (clockwise for left-handers). Now move the tube back towards the centre of the nail and stop turning and pressing. This is the first petal of the apple blossom which has five petals.

4 Repeat Steps 1 and 2, to make four more petals, starting each new petal

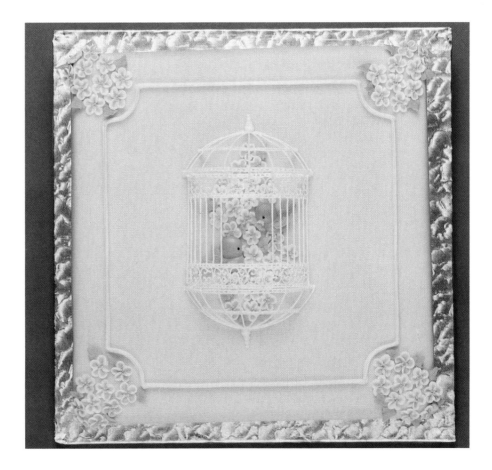

Apple blossom, Bluebirds and Blossoms, page 42

slightly under the preceding one. Take care with the last petal and lift the cone, not the tube, slightly higher, to about a 45° angle, so as not to damage the previous petals.

5 Using the cone containing the green icing, pipe five very small dots close to each other in the centre of the flower.

6 Carefully remove the waxed paper from the flower nail, holding a corner between thumb and forefinger and then sliding the middle finger underneath the paper to support the flower. Place the flower in a box or on a piece of glass to dry.

7 To make a bud, pipe three petals following the instructions for the blossom.

8 Turn the flower nail so that the three petals are upside down and facing towards you. With a small writing tube filled with green icing, pipe a teardrop starting from the base of the first petal and finishing close to the top of the petal. Repeat on the other two petals to form the calyx.

9 Turn the nail so that the petals are the right way up. Place the tube against the base of the calyx and press very firmly to form a bulb, then taper away into a stem.

● To make a smaller bud, make only two petals and do exactly the same as described above. These buds help to 'soften' the arrangement of flowers on a cake.

10 To make a leaf, fill a plain paper cone with green royal icing and cut the cone to form a leaf shape, or use a leaf tube.

11 Press firmly and allow the icing to build up. Reduce the pressure and pull

Daisies and roses, Pretty Parasol, page 128

the tube away, tapering the end of the leaf.

● These leaves can be made in advance and allowed to dry or they can be piped directly on to a cake and used to attach the royal icing flowers.

DAISY

EQUIPMENT
white royal icing (page 13)
yellow food colouring
tubes: medium petal and small writing
40-mm square waxed paper
flower nail

Two types of daisy can be piped. Before making either, follow these instructions: colour a quarter of the icing yellow. Fill a cone with a medium petal tube and white royal icing and another with a small writing tube and yellow icing. Attach a square of waxed paper to the flower nail with a dot of royal icing.

METHOD 1
1 With the medium petal tube and white icing, pipe a series of petals following the instructions for apple blossom (page 33), but making each petal slightly longer. Do not forget that the wider opening in the tube must be facing towards the centre of the nail. The daisy can have any number of petals.

2 Make a large dot in the centre of the flower using the small writing tube and yellow icing. Remove the flower and the waxed paper square from the nail and set aside to dry.

METHOD 2
1 Hold the tube containing white icing just above the surface of the nail and at right angles to it, with the wider opening in the tube towards the centre of the nail. Start about 10 mm from the centre of the nail and press firmly, moving the tube to the centre of the nail. Continue in this way, working in a circle. Any number of petals may be

piped for this flower, but they must be of even thickness and close together. Take care not to 'stretch' the icing, as this results in thin petals which break very easily when removed from the waxed paper. Do not turn the flower nail when piping a petal of this flower.

2 When the petals are complete, pipe a yellow dot in the centre of the flower using the writing tube. Remove the flower and the waxed paper from the nail and set aside to dry.

ROSE FLOWER AND BUD

EQUIPMENT
40-mm square waxed paper
flower nail
tube: large petal
pale pink royal icing (page 13)
large pin

1 Attach the waxed paper to the flower nail with a dot of royal icing. Fill a large petal tube and a paper cone with pale pink icing.

2 Hold the tube against the waxed paper on the flower nail and at right angles to it. With the wide end of the tube to the centre of the nail, press the cone, and when the icing comes through, pull the cone towards you as though you are pulling down a lever. When the side of the tube is touching the nail, turn the nail in your left hand (right, if left-handed) in a clockwise direction (anti-clockwise if left-handed), allowing the icing to wrap around the icing already on the nail, thus forming a cone.

3 Finish by turning the nail but holding the tube steady in the one position until you have completely circled the cone. Stop pressing, turn the nail and pull the tube away in the same direction, ending low on the cone and close to the nail.

4 Continue building this cone of icing by wrapping another 'band' of icing around the icing on the nail. Hold the paper cone at a 45° angle with the tube close to the top of the icing on the nail and almost touching it. This cone will form the centre of the rose. Repeat this process once more so that the cone is 15 mm high.

5 Touch the wide end of the tube to the flower cone about halfway up, with the narrow part of the tube towards your left and away from the icing. Press and turn your right hand from the wrist to the right in an 'up and over' movement, rather like opening a fan. Pipe two more petals in this way.

6 Hold the tube in the same position as for the first three petals, but start at the base of the cone, in line with the centre of the first petal, right against the nail. Move up and over, turning your hand from the wrist from left to right and finish the petal in line with the centre of the next petal of the previous row. Pipe two more petals in the same way.

7 You have now completed the rose. Carefully remove the waxed paper and rose from the nail and set aside to dry thoroughly.

8 To make a rosebud, proceed as for the rose flower, but after the first three petals shake the nail gently so that the cone falls on to its side and the 'V' formed by two of the petals is facing you.

9 Use a large pin to cut away the excess icing on either side of the base of the bud.

NOTE: The rose can be piped directly onto a cocktail stick instead of on to a flower nail.
Touch the end of the cocktail stick in some white margarine or vegetable fat and then pipe the rose directly on to it. Remove gently when the flower has set.

BLUEBIRDS

EQUIPMENT
blue royal icing (page 13)
tube: No. 0 or 1
waxed paper
tiny pieces of sponge

1 Using a No. 0 or 1 tube and blue royal icing, pipe the tail first on to waxed paper, starting with the central 'feather'. Hold the tube at a 45° angle, press, then reduce the pressure and pull towards you. Repeat this twice on each side to complete the tail.

2 Pipe two wings, one left and one right, by starting at the base. Gently press the paper cone, move outwards in a curve and then back again. Repeat twice more to complete each wing. Allow to dry.

3 Hold the paper cone at a 45° angle and press very firmly, allowing the icing to build up to form a fat round body. Reduce the pressure, move the tube up slightly and press again to form the head. Reduce the pressure again and pull away to form the beak.

4 Immediately insert the dry tail and wings into the wet body, supporting them with tiny pieces of sponge, if necessary. Allow to dry thoroughly before peeling off the waxed paper.

Part Two

An Engagement Toast

An elegant cut-out design in red decorates a white cake – ideal for a champagne celebration!

INGREDIENTS
1 × 225-mm heart-shaped cake
(page 11)
1 kg white sugarpaste (page 13)
white and red modelling paste
(page 14)
cornflour
white and red royal icing
(page 13)

**MATERIALS AND
DECORATIONS**
1 × 295-mm heart-shaped cake
board
pattern for hands and glasses
design (page 134)
craft knife
miniature heart cutter
tubes: No. 1, small and medium
fine tooth star
large pin
5/0 paintbrush
3-mm wide red satin ribbon

1 Cover the cake with white sugar-paste.

2 Roll out the white modelling paste and, using the pattern, cut out the heart shape.

3 Using the pattern, transfer the outline of the hands and glasses on to the modelling paste heart, dusting with cornflour to prevent sticking.

4 While the modelling paste is still wet, cut carefully around the outlines with the craft knife. Cut out about 15 little hearts with a miniature heart cutter. If necessary, cover part of the work with a piece of plastic to slow down the drying process.

5 Roll out the red modelling paste and, using the pattern, cut out the heart shape.

6 Position the red heart on the top of the cake, securing it with a little water.

7 Position the white heart with the cut-out design on top of the red heart, securing it with a little water.

8 Using a small fine tooth star tube and white royal icing, pipe a shell border around the heart on top of the cake.

9 Mark the position for the ribbon by holding a ruler against the sides of the cake and making a line with a large pin. Brush water over the line and attach the ribbon.

10 Make up a tiny red ribbon bow and attach to the front of the cake with royal icing.

11 Using a medium fine tooth star tube and white royal icing, pipe a shell border around the base of the cake.

12 Using a No. 1 tube and red royal icing, pipe a dot on each shell on the top and around the base of the cake.

'Will You Marry Me?'

The magic moment for sweethearts everywhere is captured in this charming design for a heart-shaped cake.

INGREDIENTS

1 × 270-mm heart-shaped cake
  (page 11)
1 kg white sugarpaste (page 13)
white, pink, grey, dark brown,
  light brown, flesh-coloured,
  black and green royal icing
  (page 13)
black and red food colouring
pink and black dusting powders
cornflour

MATERIALS AND DECORATIONS

1 × 330-mm heart-shaped board
15-mm half-round crimper
patterns for arms and umbrella
  (page 135)
pattern for boy and girl
  (page 135)
pattern for heart (page 136)
pattern for lace pieces (page 135)
tubes: Nos. 1 and 2, small
  straight petal, small star and
  leaf
waxed paper
large pin
dusting brush
22 miniature roses (page 30)

1 Cover the cake with white sugarpaste. Crimp all around the sides of the cake about 20 mm above the board with the crimper.

2 Using the patterns, flood the arms and umbrella separately on to waxed paper. Leave to dry.

3 Using royal icing and the pattern, pipe the outlines and flood the boy and girl. Leave to dry.

4 Using the pattern, trace the heart shape on to the top of the cake with a large hatpin.

5 Using the pattern, pipe 60 lace pieces, plus a few extra, on to waxed paper with a No. 1 tube and pink royal icing.

6 Complete the flooded picture by painting the eyes and mouths with food colouring, piping the girl's hair with a No. 2 tube and dark brown royal icing and the boy's with a No. 1 tube and light brown royal icing. Attach the arms with dots of royal icing.

7 With a No. 1 tube and royal icing, pipe the lines on the umbrella, the dots and leaves on the edge of dress and umbrella and the black dots on the boy's outfit, using the photograph for reference.

8 Using a small straight petal tube, pipe a pink royal icing bow directly on

to the girl's hair. Mix some pink dusting powder with a little cornflour and brush into the folds of the dress. Mix some pink and black dusting powders with a little cornflour and use to shade the boy's clothes.

9 Carefully remove the floodwork from the waxed paper and attach it to the centre of the cake with royal icing.

10 Attach the umbrella, securing it in position with royal icing.

11 Attach the lace pieces around the heart pattern on top of cake with dots of royal icing.

12 Overline the crimping with a No. 1 tube and pink royal icing.

13 Using a small star tube and white royal icing, pipe a small shell border around the base of the cake.

14 Pipe a dot on to each shell with a No. 1 tube and pink royal icing.

15 Attach a miniature rose to the bottom of umbrella, place one in the boy's hand and use four or five to make up the bunch of flowers, securing them with dots of royal icing. Attach three roses to the point of the heart shape, as shown in the photograph, and secure the remaining roses at intervals around the sides of the cake. Using a leaf tube and green royal icing, pipe leaves for the roses.

Bluebirds and Blossoms

The classic theme of two lovebirds is the inspiration for this intricately piped engagement cake.

INGREDIENTS

1 × 200 mm-square cake,
  (page 11) with cut-out corners
  (either carefully cut out
  corners of the baked cake, or
  place a quarter of an 80-mm
  diameter circular piece of
  wood of the same height as the
  cake tin in each corner of the
  tin before adding the cake
  mixture)
500 g pale blue sugarpaste
  (page 13)
pale blue, yellow, white and
  green royal icing (page 13)
pink dusting powder

MATERIALS AND DECORATIONS

1 × 250-mm square cake board
pattern for flooded bluebirds
  (page 137)
patterns for cage (page 137)
waxed paper
tubes: Nos. 0, 1, 2 and 3, leaf
  and small star
5/0 paintbrush
black food colouring
70-mm diameter curved object
  (tin or bottle)
sticky tape
permanent marker
70-mm diameter dome shape
white vegetable fat
about 50 piped pink and white
  blossoms (page 33)

1 Cover the cake with pale blue sugarpaste.

BLUEBIRDS

1 Using the pattern, pipe the partly obscured wing on to waxed paper with a No. 1 tube and pale blue royal icing and then outline the body and head. Pipe the tail as for the wing, moving the tube up and down to make consecutive lines.

2 Add a few drops of water to the blue royal icing to soften it slightly. Then use a No. 2 tube and the softened royal icing to pipe the body, brushing the icing to meet the tail but leaving the body fat and rounded.

3 Pipe the second wing separately on to waxed paper with a No. 1 tube and royal icing. Leave to dry.

4 Pipe the head with the softened royal icing, pressing firmly on the paper cone to make it full and round. Leave to dry thoroughly.

5 Pipe the beak with a No. 1 tube and yellow royal icing. Paint a small eye with black food colouring and lightly colour the cheek with pink dusting powder.

6 With a little royal icing, attach the second wing to the bird, referring to the photograph for the position. Leave to dry.

CAGE

1 Make a paper pattern of the side of the cage and attach it with sticky tape to a 70-mm diameter tin or bottle. Place a 150 × 75-mm piece of waxed paper over the pattern, attaching it with a small piece of sticky tape on each side.

2 With a No. 1 tube and white royal icing, pipe all the horizontal lines, following the pattern. Then pipe the vertical lines and leave to dry.

3 With a No. 0 tube and white royal icing, pipe the scrolls and the dots on the scrolls between the double lines. Leave to dry.

4 Remove the side of the cage by loosening the sticky tape and gently removing the waxed paper from the tin or bottle. Gently peel the paper away from the back of the icing. Place the side of the cage safely in a box.

5 Mark the outline of the pattern for the dome with a permanent marker on the 70-mm diameter dome shape.

6 Grease the dome shape lightly with white vegetable fat.

7 With white royal icing in a No. 1 tube, pipe in all the lines, starting with the central one. Leave to dry.

8 With a No. 0 tube, add the dots between the double lines and leave to dry.

9 Warm the dome slightly and very gently remove the icing shape.

10 Repeat Steps 6 to 9 to make the second dome.

TO ASSEMBLE

1 Trace a square with cut-out corners on to paper and cut out the shapes, then trace the design on to the cake with a hatpin.

2 Follow the pattern with white royal icing in a No. 3 tube. Using a No. 2 tube, pipe a line over the first line. Then, using a No. 1 tube, pipe a line over the first two. Finally, using a No. 2 tube, pipe a line inside these three lines.

3 Using the photograph for guidance, attach the blossoms to the cake with royal icing, allowing space for the bluebirds. Add the birds, positioning them on small mounds of icing. Pipe some leaves in between the blossoms with a leaf tube and green royal icing.

4 With a little royal icing, attach the side of the cage over the birds and flowers. Add the top and base domes, attaching them with royal icing.

5 Using a No. 1 tube, pipe lines from the domes to the cage body, over the gaps. Pipe four graduated dots above and below the cage to complete.

6 Attach the blossoms to the corners and the sides of the cake and pipe the leaves with a leaf tube and green royal icing.

7 Pipe shells around the base of the cake using a small star tube and white royal icing.

Springtime Wedding

A ring-shaped cake is the perfect setting for the delicate arrangement of spring flowers.

INGREDIENTS

1 × 300-mm ring-shaped cake
(page 11)
2 kg pale lemon sugarpaste
(page 13)
pale blue and lemon royal icing
(page 13)

MATERIALS AND DECORATIONS

1 × 375-mm round cake board
silver paper edging
tubes: No. 1 and small star
pattern for lace pieces (page 138)
17 apricot and lemon narcissi
(page 29)
24 small blue daisies (page 26)
9 apricot bell-shaped flowers
(page 27)
34 avocado green rose leaves
(page 172)
18 pale blue forget-me-nots,
taped in groups of 3 (page 27)
12 pale blue hyacinth buds
(page 27)
2 fluted lemon bells, moulded in
different sizes in modelling
paste
45-mm diameter scalloped
circular pastillage plaque
1 × 100-mm high pillar
5-mm wide apricot ribbon
covered fuse wire

1 Cover the cake with pale lemon sugarpaste. If necessary, cut a strip of sugarpaste for the inside of the ring after covering the rest of the cake. Cover the board with lemon sugarpaste and trim with silver paper edging.

2 With a No. 1 tube and pale blue royal icing, pipe sufficient lace pieces to fit around the base of the cake and the top of the inner circle, using the pattern.

3 Using a small star tube and lemon royal icing, pipe a shell border around the inner circle and the base of the cake.

4 Place the larger bell on top of the smaller bell to make a vase, securing them with royal icing. Leave to dry thoroughly.

5 Attach the pastillage plaque to the pillar with royal icing and leave to dry.

6 Position the pillar inside the centre of the cake and attach it to the board with royal icing.

7 Attach the lace pieces to the top of the inner circle, pointing away from the centre, as shown in the photograph. Using a No. 1 tube and pale blue royal icing, pipe a snail's trail immediately below the lace pieces.

8 Attach the lace pieces just above the shell border, around the base of the cake.

9 Make up three sprays of flowers, each consisting of three narcissi, three daisies, two bell-shaped flowers, five rose leaves, a few forget-me-nots and two hyacinth buds. Make up another three sprays, each consisting of one narcissus, two daisies and three rose leaves. Finally, make up two sprays, each consisting of one narcissus, three daisies, five rose leaves and three hyacinth buds.

10 Cut eight 300-mm lengths of ribbon, fold in half and secure with wire to form a streamer. Curl the ends with scissors. Repeat to make three more streamers.

11 Place a ball of sugarpaste inside the vase to reach about half-way up the sides. Secure with a little royal icing if necessary.

12 Insert the two longer sprays, one on each side, securing them in the sugarpaste inside the vase.

13 Secure the three shorter sprays in the sugarpaste in the front of the vase.

14 Push the ribbon loops and streamers in between the flowers.

15 Arrange the loose flowers in the vase to complete the arrangement.

16 Position the vase on the pillar, securing it with royal icing.

17 Attach three large sprays of flowers to the cake slightly to the right of the vase.

18 Add ribbons between the sprays to complete the design.

Hearts and Flowers

Three heart-shaped, pink cakes – attractively presented on cutaway stands – are unashamedly romantic.

INGREDIENTS

1 × 270-mm heart-shaped cake (page 11)
2 × 230-mm heart-shaped cakes (page 11)
2 kg very pale salmon pink sugarpaste (page 13)
white royal icing (page 13)
silver powder
caramel oil flavouring

MATERIALS AND DECORATIONS

1 × 330-mm heart-shaped cake board
2 × 290-mm heart-shaped cake boards
tubes: Nos. 0 and 1, and small fine tooth star
pattern for embroidery design for sides of cake (page 138)
pattern for shaped oval plaque with letters and embroidery (page 138)
5/0 paintbrush
4 full shaded salmon pink roses (page 29)
8 half-open shaded salmon pink roses (page 29)
4 salmon pink rose buds (page 29)
20 white mock orange blossoms (page 28)
32 pale blue bell-shaped flowers (page 27)
10 moss green daisy leaves
white ribbon
small piece of sponge
silver paper edging
2 × 200-mm high acrylic cutaway stands
1 × 50-mm high acrylic cutaway stand

1 Cover the cakes and boards with salmon pink sugarpaste.

2 Embroider the designs for the sides of the cakes with a No. 0 tube, following the pattern. Paint the design with silver powder mixed with a few drops of caramel oil flavouring.

3 To make the oval plaque, pipe the shaped oval design and appropriate letters on to a piece of acrylic or glass with a No. 0 tube and royal icing, following the instructions on page 22.

4 Roll out the white modelling paste and press the glass stencil on to it. Cut out around the outline and leave the plaque to dry thoroughly.

5 Flood the letters with royal icing and allow to dry thoroughly. Using a No. 1 tube, pipe a single line of white royal icing on to each letter and around edge of the plaque. Paint over the lines with silver.

6 Using a No. 0 tube and white royal icing, embroider the design on to the shaped oval. Paint the design with silver.

7 Make up four sprays of flowers with ribbon as follows: two sprays, each consisting of one full rose, one half-open rose, one rose bud, five mock orange blossoms, seven bell-shaped flowers and three daisy leaves; two sprays, each consisting of one full rose, three half-open roses, one rose bud, five mock orange blossoms, nine bell-shaped flowers and two daisy leaves.

8 Pipe a small shell border in white royal icing around the base of each cake, using a small fine tooth star tube.

9 Using a No. 1 tube and white royal icing, pipe dots 15 mm apart around base of each cake, about 10 mm above the board. Pipe loops from the first dot to the third and then from the second dot to the fourth. Continue all around the cake in this way.

10 Attach the flower sprays to the tops of the cakes as shown in the photograph, using royal icing.

11 Attach the shaped oval plaque to top of the largest heart-shaped cake using dots of royal icing and support with a piece of sponge until set.

12 Attach the silver paper edging around the boards to finish them off.

13 Position the completed cakes on the acrylic cutaway stands.

His and Hers

A top hat and picture hat provide a witty alternative to the traditional wedding cake.

INGREDIENTS
2 × 150-mm round cakes
    (page 11)
1 × 200-mm round cake
    (page 11)
1 kg white sugarpaste (page 13)
1 kg grey sugarpaste (page 13)
500 g white modelling paste
    (page 14)
grey food colouring
white and grey royal icing
    (page 13)

MATERIALS AND DECORATIONS
1 × 250-mm round cake board
1 × 400-mm round cake board
piece of sponge
1 × 175-mm diameter paper
    circle marked into 4
1 × 400-mm diameter paper
    circle marked into 4
1 × 250-mm diameter paper
    circle marked into 4
tubes: Nos. 1 and 2
7 thin cardboard cones, to
    support the brim of the picture
    hat
pattern for eyelet embroidery
    (page 138)
39 small mimosa flowers, taped
    in groups of 3 (page 28)
8 small white daisies (page 26)
9 medium-sized yellow daisies
    (page 26)
9 medium-sized apricot daisies
    (page 26)
5-mm wide yellow and apricot
    ribbons
1 × 200-mm high acrylic
    cutaway stand
1 × 50-mm high acrylic cutaway
    stand

TOP HAT

1 Mix together 250 g of the white sugarpaste and 250 g of the white modelling paste and colour to match the grey sugarpaste.

2 Roll out this mixture and cut out a 250-mm circle. Place the circle on the 250-mm round board and prop up with a piece of sponge to shape.

3 Place the two 150-mm round cakes on top of each other. Fill in any gaps between the cakes with marzipan and spread with smooth apricot jam.

4 Roll out a grey sugarpaste rectangle of 150 × 500 mm. Place the joined cakes on their side and roll the sugarpaste around them, smoothing carefully.

5 Roll out the grey sugarpaste and cut out a 175-mm diameter circle for the top of the hat. Attach and smooth by rubbing gently with your hand.

6 Place the cakes on the shaped circle/hat brim.

7 Cut two lengths of apricot and one length of yellow ribbon to go around the hat and secure them with dots of royal icing.

8 Using a No. 2 tube and grey royal icing, pipe a snail's trail around the crown and edge of brim.

PICTURE HAT

1 Mix together 250 g white modelling paste and 500 g white sugarpaste and set aside for the brim of the hat.

2 Centre the 200-mm round cake on the large cake board and cover with white sugarpaste.

3 Roll out the white modelling paste and sugarpaste mixture, rolling it more thinly towards the outer edge.

4 Cut out a 400-mm diameter circle from this mixture and mark the centre. Cut out a 175-mm diameter circle from the centre of the circle.

5 Lift the outer circle over the cake and down on to the cake board.

6 Lift the circle at intervals to create the brim, supporting it with cardboard cones.

7 Immediately cut out the eyelet embroidery design around the brim, using the pattern. Using a No. 1 tube and white royal icing, pipe around each opening. Embroider dots and leaves between the openings, as shown in the photograph.

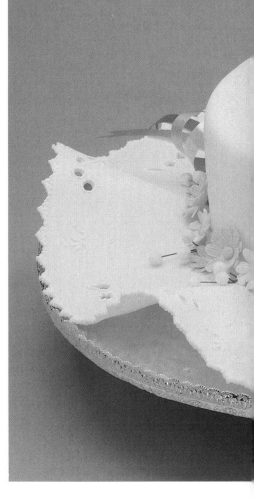

8 Position some of the daisies against the hat while they are still damp, fitting them snugly against the hat and brim.

9 Arrange the remaining daisies and the mimosa sprays around brim of the hat, attaching them with royal icing.

10 Trim the edge of the brim with a picot edge made from white royal icing, following the instructions on page 21, using a No. 2 tube for the first row of dots and a No. 1 tube for the subsequent rows.

11 Add a ribbon bow and two lengths of ribbon at the back of the hat.

12 Position the cakes on the stands.

Azalea Bouquet

Simply stunning — an interesting shape is created by using two hexagonal cakes, linked by an elegant bouquet.

INGREDIENTS

2 × 225-mm hexagonal cakes
    (page 11)
1.5 kg white sugarpaste (page 13)
maroon royal icing (page 13)

MATERIALS AND DECORATIONS

2 cake boards (any shape)
tubes: Nos. 1, 2 and 3
2 × 180-mm hexagonal dummies
2 × 180-mm hexagonal pieces of
    waxed paper
large pin
500 × 340-mm rectangular cake
    board
frill ruler
6 azaleas (page 24)
10 small pink daphne (page 27)
12 medium-sized pink daphne
    (page 27)
16 large pink daphne (page 27)
24 small white daphne, touched
    with maroon (page 27)
8 pink hyacinth buds (page 27)

1 Using any cake boards, cover the cakes with white sugarpaste. Ensure that the cakes do not stick to the boards so that they can be moved around. Leave to set firm for about 72 hours.

2 Using a No. 1 tube and maroon royal icing, pipe dots 15 mm apart around five of the top edges of each cake.

3 Place a dummy and a hexagonal piece of waxed paper on each cake, centring carefully. Mark around the dummy on the icing with a large pin. Hold the cake, board and dummy between your hands and carefully turn them all over and position them so that you can follow the next step.

4 Using a No. 1 tube and maroon royal icing, pipe three loops of different lengths from the first dot to the third. Pipe three loops from the second to the fourth dot, and so on around the cake. Repeat on the second cake.

5 Cover the rectangular board with white sugarpaste and mark the exact positions of the cakes. (Cake shapes can be cut out of the icing if desired.) Turn the cakes over and carefully position on the board.

6 Using a frill ruler or scalloped template, mark scallops on to the sugarpaste around the cake bases.

7 Make up two sprays of flowers, each consisting of three azaleas, two small pink daphne, three medium-sized pink daphne, eight large pink daphne, nine small white daphne, touched with maroon and three pink hyacinth buds. Make up two more sprays of flowers, each consisting of three small pink daphne, three medium-sized pink daphne, three small white daphne, touched with maroon, and one pink hyacinth bud.

8 Using a No. 2 tube and maroon royal icing, pipe over the scalloped markings close to the base of the cakes.

9 Pipe beads around bases of the cakes using a No. 3 tube and white royal icing.

10 Using a No. 2 tube and white royal icing, pipe a snail's trail around the hexagonal marks on the top of each cake and around the edges of the boards.

11 Carefully attach the flower sprays to the tops of the cakes with dots of royal icing.

Butterflies, Rings and Daisies

Multi-coloured daisy chains encircle the three wedding cakes, all decorated with butterflies.

INGREDIENTS
1 × 200-mm round cake
   (page 11)
2 × 225-mm round cakes
   (page 11)
2.5 kg pale pink sugarpaste
   (page 13)
50 g pale pink pastillage
   (page 15)
white royal icing (page 13)

MATERIALS AND DECORATIONS
1 × 250-mm round cake board
2 × 275-mm round cake boards
20 medium-sized pink daisies
   (page 26)
20 medium-sized dusty pink
   daisies (page 26)
20 medium-sized mauve daisies
   (page 26)
45 small pink daisies (page 26)
45 small dusty pink daisies
   (page 26)
45 small mauve daisies (page 26)
6 pink butterflies, shaded with
   violet and pink (page 32)
45-mm diameter jars
tubes: No. 1 and small star
cotton wool or small piece of
   sponge
1 × 200-mm high acrylic stand
2 × 50-mm high acrylic stands

---

1 Cover the cakes and boards with pale pink sugarpaste.

2 Roll out the pink pastillage and cut into two 130-mm long strips, 3-mm wide. Secure the strips around the small jars to set into rings and allow to dry thoroughly.

3 Using a No. 1 tube and white royal icing, pipe dots at intervals over each cake, using the photograph for reference.

4 Using a small star tube and white royal icing, pipe a shell border around the edge of each board.

5 Attach the medium-sized daisies in a circle around the top edge of each cake, using dots of royal icing. Attach the small daisies around the base of each cake.

6 Overlap the two rings and attach them to each other with royal icing. Support them with cotton wool or a small piece of sponge until dry.

7 Attach the rings to the small cake with royal icing and leave to set.

8 Attach a butterfly to each ring with a dot of royal icing.

9 Attach a pair of butterflies to each of the two larger cakes.

10 Position the cakes on the stands, as shown in the photograph.

Detail of butterflies and rings

Horse and Carriage

A romantic means of transport for the bridal couple to use on their wedding day.

INGREDIENTS
250 × 200-mm oval cake
  (page 11)
1 kg pale blue sugarpaste
  (page 13)
white pastillage or modelling
  paste (page 15, or page 14)
white royal icing (page 13)

MATERIALS AND DECORATIONS
300 × 250-mm oval cake board
10-mm half-round crimper
patterns for horses and carriage
  (page 139)
waxed paper
tubes: Nos. 0, 1 and 2, and small
  star

1 Cover the cake with pale blue sugarpaste and immediately crimp the top edge using the half-round crimper.

2 Roll out the white pastillage or modelling paste and cut out the horses, using the pattern.

3 Pipe the carriage wheels on to waxed paper using a No. 2 tube and white royal icing for the outlines and a No. 1 tube for the inside spokes and other details. Fill in the centres of the wheels using a No. 1 tube with royal icing which has been softened with a few drops of water.

4 Pipe the carriage outline and scrolls with a No. 1 tube on to waxed paper.

5 Pipe the trellis on the door and the side of the carriage with a No. 0 tube and then overline with a No. 0 tube.

6 The dickey is outlined with a No. 2 tube and the trellis and scrolls are piped with a No. 1 tube.

7 Pipe a mane, tail and harness on one side of each horse using a No. 1 tube.

8 Trace the outline of the carriage on to the cake.

9 Using dots of royal icing, attach the front and back wheels, referring to the photograph for guidance on position.

10 Attach one horse in the correct position, using royal icing.

11 Pipe three lines with a No. 2 tube one on top of the other over the outlines for the carriage and dickey and over the shaft between the horses. Leave to dry.

12 Gently peel the piped carriage off the waxed paper.

13 Pipe an additional line with a No. 2 tube over the carriage outline on the cake and immediately place the piped carriage on top of this line, pressing gently to secure.

14 Repeat Step 13 with the dickey.

15 Pipe a line with a No. 2 tube over the shaft on top of the first horse and attach the second horse on top of this line.

16 Attach the second set of two wheels by building up an axle in royal icing using a No. 2 tube.

17 Overline the crimping with a No. 1 tube.

18 Pipe a dot at each point of the crimping on the top of the cake.

19 Pipe three graduated dots on the side of the cake below the points of the crimping, referring to the photograph for guidance.

20 Using a small star tube, pipe a shell border around the base of the cake.

21 Pipe the reins from the dickey to the horses using a No. 1 tube and white royal icing.

Silver Celebration

This unusual cutaway cake, with elaborate pink and white filigree cornerpieces, is ideal for a silver wedding party.

INGREDIENTS

1 × 200-mm square cake,
  60-mm high (page 11)
1 kg white sugarpaste (page 13)
pale pink and white royal icing
  (page 13)
silver powder
caramel oil flavouring

MATERIALS AND DECORATIONS

1 × 250-mm square thick board
1 × 120-mm square thin board
patterns for filigree work
  (page 140)
pattern for lettering (page 171)
pattern for numerals (page 140)
waxed paper
tubes: Nos. 1 and 2, and small
  fine tooth star
5/0 paintbrush
small pieces of sponge
80-mm high × 60-mm diameter
  acrylic stand

1 Cut a 100-mm square out of one corner of the cake and place it on the thin board, leaving the balance of the cake on the 250-mm square board.

2 Make a glass stencil of the message, following the instructions on page 22.

3 Cover both cakes with white sugarpaste, ensuring the icing is taken right down to the boards.

4 Immediately the cakes have been covered, press the stencil across one corner of the large cake, referring to the photograph for guidance.

5 Using the patterns and referring to the photograph for guidance, pipe six Part A and six Part B filigree pieces on to waxed paper, using No. 1 tubes and white and pink royal icing. Pipe white dots as shown and then paint them with silver powder mixed with a few drops of caramel oil flavouring.

6 Pipe the message in white royal icing, using a No. 1 tube. When dry, paint with silver.

7 Using white royal icing and the pattern, flood the numerals on to waxed paper and leave to dry.

8 Carefully remove the filigree pieces from the waxed paper. Attach two corner pieces to the small cake by piping a line on to the back corner on the top of the cake. Support them with small pieces of sponge and leave to dry.

9 Attach the remaining filigree pieces to the relevant corners, referring to the photograph.

10 Paint the floodwork numerals with silver and remove them from the waxed paper. Attach the numerals to the cake with small dots of royal icing and support them with small pieces of sponge until dry.

11 Pipe two lines in royal icing on the front corner of the top of the small cake, as shown in the photograph. Pipe the outer line with a No. 2 tube and the inner line with a No. 1 tube. Paint the lines with silver.

12 Pipe two lines on the back of the larger cake in the same way, using white royal icing. Paint the lines with silver.

13 Using a No. 2 tube and white royal icing, pipe a snail's trail at the base of each cake, between the filigree pieces.

14 Using a small fine tooth star tube and white royal icing, pipe a shell border around the base of each cake.

15 Position the small cake on the acrylic stand in the cut-out corner of the large cake, as shown in the photograph.

Detail of filigree work and numerals

It's Our Day!

For that special anniversary, an exquisite arrangement of orchids, carnations and trailing ivy.

INGREDIENTS

1 × 250-mm round cake
(page 11)
1 kg cream sugarpaste (page 13)
cream royal icing (page 13)

MATERIALS AND DECORATIONS

1 × 300-mm round cake board
tubes: No. 2 and two sizes of star
10-mm wide cream ribbon
18 small ivy leaves (page 27)
14 medium-sized ivy leaves
(page 27)
9 large ivy leaves (page 27)
2 cream cymbidium orchids
(page 25)
7 very small pale pink carnations
(page 25)
15 very small white bell-shaped
flowers, taped in groups of 3
(page 27)
1 peach-coloured candle (about
130 mm high)

1 Cover the cake and board with cream sugarpaste.

2 Using a No. 2 tube and cream royal icing, pipe dots at 10-mm intervals around the top of the cake.

3 Using a No. 2 tube and cream royal icing, pipe loops around the top of the cake, piping from the first to the fourth dot and then the second to the fifth dot, and so on.

4 Using the larger star tube and cream royal icing, pipe a shell border around the base of the cake.

5 Secure ribbon all around the edge of the board.

6 Pipe a shell border all around the edge of the board, using cream royal icing in the smaller star tube.

7 Make up five sprays of ivy leaves, using a combination of small, medium-sized and large leaves for each.

8 Attach a small piece of cream sugarpaste to the top of the cake, using a little water.

9 Arrange the orchids, sprays of ivy, carnations and bell-shaped flowers on the top of the cake, securing them in the sugarpaste.

10 Attach the candle with a little royal icing and, if necessary, add ribbon bows behind the arrangement to neaten.

Detail of ivy spray

Happy Anniversary

The exotic green cymbidium orchid is framed by small pink flowers on this scalloped oval cake.

Detail of ribbon insertion and frill

1 Cover the cake with sugarpaste.

2 Using the pattern, insert ribbons in the sides of the cake about 25 mm apart and 45 mm above the cake board.

3 Using the pattern, mark the positions of the three frills around the cake with a large pin.

4 Embroider between the ribbon insertion in salmon pink and lime green royal icing with a No. 0 tube, using the pattern.

5 Attach frills made of white modelling paste to the cake, starting from the bottom and using the photograph for guidance.

6 Using a No. 1 tube and white royal icing, edge the top frill with a snail's trail.

7 Make up two sprays of flowers, each consisting of seven salmon pink primulas and three lime green buds. Make up two more sprays, each consisting of four salmon pink primulas and three lime green buds.

8 Make up three ribbon bows.

9 Attach the orchid, flower sprays and ribbon bows to the top of the cake with dots of royal icing, using the photograph for reference.

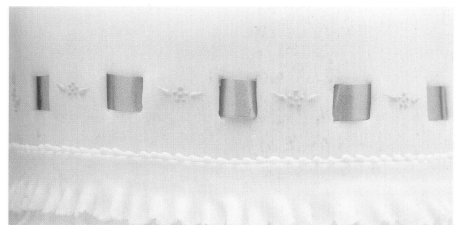

Blue for a Boy

This novel design for a christening cake can be adapted for a baby girl by using pink instead of blue.

INGREDIENTS

1 × 225-mm round cake
(page 11)
pale blue and pale lemon royal
icing (page 13)
1 kg pale blue sugarpaste
(page 13)
blue and lemon food colourings
for airbrushing
pale blue and white modelling
paste (page 14)
pale blue, lemon yellow, brown
and flesh-coloured dusting
powders

MATERIALS AND DECORATIONS

1 × 250-mm round cake board
pattern for collar (page 142)
pattern for plaque (page 141)
pattern for picture of baby
(page 141)
pattern for bow (page 142)
waxed paper
275-mm square paper grid, cut
with 20-mm panels
airbrush
tubes: Nos. 1, 2 and 3

1 Cover the cake and board with pale blue sugarpaste.

2 Using the pattern provided, flood the collar with pale blue royal icing on waxed paper. Leave to dry.

3 Place the paper grid on the top of the cake and airbrush blue over the grid vertically across the cake. Gently move the grid 10 mm to the right and airbrush with lemon.

4 Turn the grid in a clockwise direction until it is possible to airbrush blue horizontal lines across the cake. Move the grid 10 mm upwards and then airbrush with lemon.

5 Roll out the white modelling paste and, using the pattern, cut out the plaque.

6 Transfer the picture of the baby on to the plaque.

7 Colour the picture with the dusting powders, using the photograph for reference.

8 Using a No. 2 tube and lemon royal icing, pipe the name on the plaque. Overpipe, using a No. 1 tube.

9 Attach the plaque to the centre of the cake with royal icing.

10 Using a No. 3 tube and pale blue royal icing, pipe rattles on the sides of the cake. Pipe lemon bows on the rattles with royal icing in a No. 1 tube.

11 Gently remove the collar from the waxed paper. Attach it to the top of the cake with dots of pale blue royal icing.

12 Make up the bow from pale blue modelling paste, using the pattern.

13 Attach the bow to the top of the cake with dots of royal icing.

Detail of collar, plaque, rattlers and components of bow

Twin Blessings

Two prettily decorated cakes to celebrate the christening of twin baby girls.

INGREDIENTS

2 × 150-mm round cakes
  (page 11)
1 kg pale green sugarpaste
  (page 13)
pale pink, green and white royal
  icing (page 13)
white modelling paste (page 14)
cornflour
silver powder
caramel oil flavouring
pink dusting powder

MATERIALS AND DECORATIONS

1 × 380 × 280-mm rectangular
  cake board
crimper
pattern for position of ribbon
  insertion (page 143)
pattern for lace pieces (page 143)
pattern for quilt (page 143)
tubes: Nos. 1 and 2
egg mould (2 halves)
6 large pink primulas (page 27)
12 small pink primulas (page 27)
10 small white daphne (page 27)
6 white hyacinth buds (page 27)
10-mm wide pink ribbon
scalloped circle cutter
5/0 paintbrush
anger tool
2 babies' heads (page 32)

1 Cover the cakes with pale green sugarpaste. Position the cakes on the board.

2 Crimp the top edges of both cakes.

3 Using the pattern, insert the ribbon around each cake (page 22), half-way up the side of the cake. Using a No. 1 tube and pale pink royal icing, embroider in the gaps between ribbons, following the pattern.

4 Overline the crimping with a No. 1 tube and pale pink royal icing.

5 Using a No. 2 tube and pale pink royal icing, pipe a snail's trail around the base of each cake.

6 To make the cradle, roll out the white modelling paste and brush cornflour on the reverse side. Shape over one half of the egg mould and cut away excess modelling paste. Leave to set firm, moving the cradle slightly every few minutes to ensure it does not stick to the mould.

7 To make the hood of the cradle, repeat Step 6 using the other half of the mould. Cut the moulded egg-shape in half while still wet and discard the bottom half.

8 Using the pattern, pipe 50 lace pieces with a No. 1 tube and pink royal icing.

9 Make up two sprays of flowers, each consisting of three large pink primulas, six small pink primulas, five small white daphne and three white hyacinth buds. Add pink ribbon bows.

10 Cut out two 'ribbons' of white modelling paste, 18 mm wide and 130 mm long. Cut out a small triangle from each end and shape the 'ribbons' as shown in the photograph. Pipe an appropriate name on each ribbon using a No. 1 tube and white royal icing. Paint the names with silver powder mixed with a few drops of caramel oil flavouring.

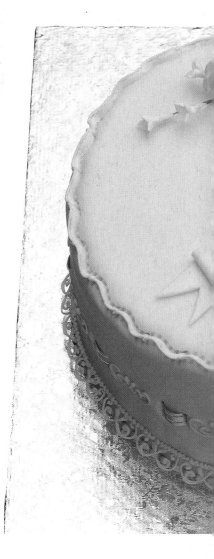

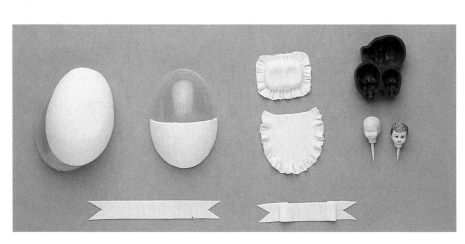

11 Attach the lace pieces with a line of pink royal icing piped with a No. 1 tube. Finish off above the pieces with a row of dots.

12 Using the pattern, cut out the frills for the top edge of the cradle hood and the sides of cradle from white modelling paste. Shape the frills with the anger tool, attach them to the cradle with a little water or royal icing and tint them with pink dusting powder, as shown in the photograph.

13 Roll two sausages of modelling paste for the babies' bodies, ensuring that they fit in the cradle.

14 Roll out a thick piece of modelling paste for the mattress and place in the cradle. Secure with royal icing.

15 Make up the pillow as shown in the photograph. Make two dents in the pillow for the babies' heads. Brush the frill of the pillow with pink dusting powder and position it in the cradle.

16 Position the babies' heads and bodies in the cradle, securing them with royal icing.

17 Roll out some modelling paste and, using the pattern, cut out the quilt. Using a knife, mark with a diamond pattern. Frill the edges using the anger tool and brush with dusting powder.

18 Using a No. 1 tube, pipe dots of pink and green royal icing on the quilt to represent tiny roses.

Sophisticated Lady

The open fan with a spray of sweet peas on this elegant cake make it a spectacular design for a midsummer birthday party.

INGREDIENTS

1 × 250-mm round cake
    (page 11)
1 kg white sugarpaste (page 13)
lilac and pink food colouring for
    airbrushing
lilac modelling paste (page 14)
white and lilac royal icing
    (page 13)

MATERIALS AND DECORATIONS

1 × 330-mm round cake board
paper strip to fit exactly around
    the side of the cake
pattern for side of cake
    (page 144)
pattern for fan (page 144)
pattern for embroidery (page 144)
sticky tape
airbrush
tubes: No. 0 and small star
10-mm wide lilac ribbon
anger tool
clear plastic sheet (about 300-mm
    square)
3 lilac sweet peas (page 30)
4 dark pink sweet peas (page 30)
2 pale pink sweet peas (page 30)
5 moss green sweet pea leaves
    (page 30)
4 sweet pea tendrils (page 30)

1 Cover the cake and board with white sugarpaste.

2 Cut the paper strip as shown in the pattern, wrap it closely around the cake and secure with sticky tape. Cover the board with a paper circle and lay another paper circle on top of the cake, covering it completely.

3 Use an airbrush to spray lilac food colouring evenly over the pattern around the cake.

4 Move the pattern carefully 10 mm around the cake and spray again with pink food colouring to create stripes, as shown in the photograph.

5 Roll out the lilac modelling paste and cut out 11 fan sections, using the pattern. Allow to dry.

6 With a No. 1 tube and white royal icing, embroider the fan sections, using the pattern.

7 Assemble the fan by threading the ribbon through the sections. Secure the ends of the ribbon with royal icing where necessary.

8 Roll out the white modelling paste and cut out a 300-mm diameter circle. Frill the edges with an anger tool, covering the circle with the plastic square to prevent it from drying and lifting the plastic as necessary while frilling.

9 Cut out a 250-mm diameter circle from the centre of the 300-mm diameter circle. Trim away an additional 5 mm from the centre to allow it to fit over the cake.

10 Carefully lower the circle over the cake and down on to the board. Attach it to the board with royal icing.

11 Repeat Steps 8 and 9 with a 250-mm diameter outer circle and 200-mm diameter inner circle. Repeat Steps 8 and 9 with a 275-mm diameter outer circle and a 225-mm diameter inner circle. Allow both circular frills to set firm on a level surface.

12 Using royal icing, attach the two circular frills to the top of the cake.

13 Using a small star tube and lilac royal icing, pipe a shell border around the base of the cake, along the top edge and around the inside of the top frills.

14 Attach the fan to the top of the cake using royal icing and supporting it with a small piece of modelling paste.

15 Make up a spray of sweet peas, leaves and tendrils and attach it to the top of the cake with dots of royal icing, as shown.

Horn of Plenty

With its basket weave horn and realistic moulded fruit, this cake makes an excellent centrepiece for a celebration buffet.

INGREDIENTS

1 × 200-mm square cake
(page 11)
750 g pale lemon sugarpaste
(page 13)
light brown, green, red, yellow
and orange modelling paste
(page 14)
light brown and lemon royal icing
(page 13)
yellow, green and brown food
colourings

MATERIALS AND DECORATIONS

1 × 250-mm square cake board
10-mm half-round crimper
waxed paper
tubes: No. 1 and small star
old-fashioned grater
pointed modelling tool
pattern for rose leaf (page 172)

1 Cover the cake with pale lemon sugarpaste.

2 Using a half-round crimper, crimp around the top edge of the cake.

3 Using light brown modelling paste and referring to the photograph for guidance, mould the horn and allow it to dry.

4 Place the horn on waxed paper and, using a small star tube and light brown royal icing, pipe basket weave (page 21) all over the horn, as shown. Leave to dry.

5 Using the photograph for reference, mould the modelling paste fruit and nuts. Three bananas, three small green apples, two large red apples, two oranges, one pear, a bunch of green grapes and three nuts are needed. Use the grater and modelling tool to shape and give texture to the fruit and nuts, adding details with food colourings.

6 Using the pattern and green modelling paste, mould two leaves and cut out three miniature stars for the strawberry calyxes.

7 Pipe the pips on the strawberries with a No. 1 tube and lemon royal icing.

8 Using a No. 1 tube and light brown royal icing, overpipe the crimping around the top edge of the cake and then pipe dots on the sides of the cake as shown in the photograph.

9 Using a small star tube and light brown royal icing, pipe a shell border around the base of the cake.

10 Position the horn on the top of the cake and attach with royal icing.

11 Arrange the fruit and nuts as shown, and attach them to the cake with royal icing.

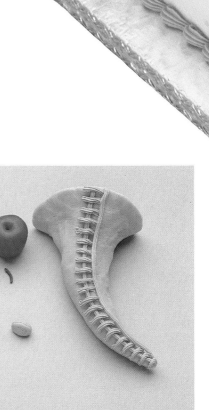

Detail of moulded horn, fruit and nuts

Lavender Lady

Scalloped frills and miniature bows surround the moulded figure on this decidedly romantic oval cake.

INGREDIENTS
1 × 200 × 170-mm oval cake
   (page 11)
750 g lavender sugarpaste
   (page 13)
250 g white sugarpaste (page 13)
cornflour
flesh-coloured and lavender
   dusting powders
white and light brown royal icing
   (page 13)
brown and pink food colourings
100 g white modelling paste
   (page 14)

MATERIALS AND DECORATIONS
1 × 255 × 220-mm oval cake
   board
crinoline lady mould
tubes: Nos. 1 and 2
5/0 paintbrush
strip of greaseproof paper to fit
   around side of cake
large pin
circular frill cutters
anger tool

1 Cover the cake and board with lavender sugarpaste.

2 Roll the white sugarpaste into a ball and then into a sausage shape. Rub cornflour on the outside of the sugarpaste and press it into the mould. Press down very firmly to ensure good detail and remove quickly from the mould.

3 Place the sugarpaste figure on a flat surface and brush the face and hands with flesh-coloured dusting powder. Then brush the parasol and frills with lavender dusting powder.

4 Using a No. 1 tube and white royal icing, trim the parasol and dress with dots, and the brim of the hat with scallops, as shown in the photograph. Use a No. 2 tube and white royal icing to trim the bottom of the dress with scallops.

5 Using a No. 1 tube and light brown royal icing, pipe the lady's hair.

6 Paint on the features with brown and pink food colouring.

7 Attach the moulded figure to the top of the cake with royal icing.

8 Fold the strip of greaseproof paper into six and mark a scallop on each section. Cut out the scallop.

9 Secure the scalloped strip around the cake and, using a large pin, mark in the scallops.

10 Roll out the white modelling paste and cut out a scalloped circle with frill cutters, using the greaseproof paper pattern for guidance. Cut out a smaller scalloped circle from the centre.

11 Frill the larger circle with the anger tool. Cut the circle to open it. Attach the frill to the cake with water or royal icing.

12 Repeat Steps 10 and 11 to make five more frills.

13 Using a No. 1 tube and white royal icing, pipe dots along the top of each frill.

14 Using a No. 1 tube and white royal icing, pipe a snail's trail along the base of the cake and around the edge of the cake board.

15 Roll out the white modelling paste and cut out six miniature bows. Using royal icing, attach these to the points of the frills, as shown in the photograph. Cut out three slightly smaller bows and attach them to the front of the dress.

Detail of moulded figure

A Basket of Flowers

The intricate piping around the edges of this cake complements the graceful basket on the top.

INGREDIENTS

1 × 175-mm round cake
   (page 11)
500 g white sugarpaste (page 13)
golden-yellow, pale green and
   white royal icing (page 13)
pale pink, white and green
   modelling paste (page 14)

MATERIALS AND DECORATIONS

1 × 225-mm round cake board
pattern for basket (page 145)
tubes: Nos. 1 and 2, and medium
   star
flower cutters
leaf cutters
ball tool

1 Cover the cake with white sugar-paste.

2 Using the pattern, trace the basket on to the cake.

3 For the upper edge of the basket, use a No. 2 tube and golden-yellow royal icing. First pipe a short line of about 2 cm along the centre of the top of the basket. Pipe a line on top of that measuring 3 cm, and then subsequent lines one on top of the other measuring 4 cm and 6 cm. The base of the basket is also piped in this manner, starting with a short line and then two progressively longer lines over the top.

4 Pipe the roping (page 23) for the handle with a No. 2 tube and golden-yellow royal icing.

5 Using a No. 2 tube and golden-yellow royal icing, pipe the scalloped edge of the basket, building it up with four or five lines of icing.

6 Pipe the main vertical lines of the basket with a No. 2 tube and golden-yellow icing. Pipe two lines on top of each other to form the sides of the basket, building higher towards the centre with three, four and five lines of icing.

7 Pipe two lines with a No. 2 tube over the length of the top of the basket.

8 Using a No. 1 tube and golden-yellow icing, pipe the trelliswork on the sides of the basket, using the photograph for guidance. Neaten the vertical lines by overpiping with a No. 1 tube.

9 With a No. 1 tube and pale green royal icing, pipe dots around the top edge of the cake at 15-mm intervals, as shown.

10 With a No. 1 tube and pale green royal icing, pipe loops from dot to dot.

11 With a No. 1 tube and pale green royal icing, pipe a teardrop with a curved teardrop on either side to form a *fleur-de-lis* in alternate spaces, as shown.

12 Using a medium star tube and white royal icing, pipe pull-up shells around the base of the cake.

13 With a No. 1 tube and pale green royal icing, pipe loops at the base of the cake, using the photograph for reference.

14 Using flower and leaf cutters and a ball tool, mould the flowers and leaves from modelling paste, as shown.

15 Position the flowers in the basket, using the photograph for guidance, and attach them with royal icing.

Detail of flowers

Once upon a Time

Sure to be a winner at children's parties, this colourful fantasy cake depicts delightful storybook characters.

INGREDIENTS

1 × 330 × 250-mm book-shaped sponge cake (page 12), made in a book-shaped or rectangular tin and built up with sugarpaste

white, brown, green, red, flesh-coloured, yellow, pink and blue royal icing (page 13)

pink, white, yellow, orange, beige, brown and pale green modelling paste (page 14)

100 g blue modelling paste (page 14)

100 g blue sugarpaste (page 13)

1.5 kg white sugarpaste (page 13)

green, brown and blue airbrush food colourings or dusting powders

black food colouring

MATERIALS AND DECORATIONS

patterns for pixies, fairies and butterfly, animals and birds (page 146)

waxed paper

blossom cutter

ball tool

tubes: Nos. 1, 2 and 3, small star and small leaf

1 × 380 × 280-mm cake board

ruler

airbrush, if desired

5/0 paintbrush

additional small paper cones

1 Using the patterns and referring to the photograph for guidance on colour, flood the fairy story characters on to waxed paper. Leave to dry thoroughly.

2 Roll out the pink modelling paste and cut out the blossoms, using the blossom cutter. Hollow them with a ball tool and add a yellow dot of royal icing in the centre of each with a No. 1 tube.

3 Combine the 100 g blue modelling paste and 100 g blue sugarpaste and roll the mixture into a long sausage shape to fit all around the edge of the cake board. Roll outwards, forming a border around the edge of the board to serve as the cover of the book. The border should be about 30 mm wide.

4 Place the cake on the board and cover it with white sugarpaste. Use a ruler to press against the sides of the cake to create the effect of pages.

5 Use the airbrush to spray green and brown food colouring on the lower part of the pages and blue on the top for the sky, or use dusting powders to create a similar effect.

6 With a No. 3 tube and brown royal icing, pipe stems and branches on to the cake, as shown in the photograph.

7 Paint the features on the fairy story characters with black food colouring.

8 Remove the floodwork figures from the waxed paper. Attach the figures with royal icing, referring to the photograph for guidance on position.

9 Attach the blossoms to the branches with royal icing.

10 Pipe the nest on the branches with a No. 2 tube and brown royal icing.

11 With a small leaf tube and green royal icing in a paper cone, pipe leaves on to the branches and between figures and flowers, as shown.

12 Mould the present, bow and tag from modelling paste, using the photograph for reference.

13 Mould toadstools in modelling paste, as shown in the photograph. Attach the toadstools to the cake, as shown, and position the present on a toadstool, attaching it with royal icing.

14 Using a small star tube and blue royal icing, pipe a shell border around the edge of the book cover.

Ballet Shoes

Moulded ballet shoes and floodwork ballerinas decorate this pretty cake for a young ballet enthusiast.

INGREDIENTS
1 × 200-mm round cake (page 11)
750 g sky blue sugarpaste (page 13)
sky blue, white, pink, flesh-coloured and brown royal icing (page 13)
pink modelling paste (page 14)
sky blue pastillage (page 15)
black food colouring

MATERIALS AND DECORATIONS
1 × 300-mm round cake board
patterns for ballerinas (page 145)
waxed paper
tubes: Nos. 1 and 2
4 miniature pink roses (page 30)
8 miniature half-open pink roses (page 30)
8 miniature pink rose buds (page 30)
silver paper edging

1 Cover the cake with sky blue sugarpaste.

2 Flood the cake board with sky blue royal icing. Leave to dry thoroughly.

3 Using pink modelling paste, mould the ballet shoes, either freehand or in a mould. Refer to the photograph for guidance.

4 Using the patterns, flood two of each ballerina on to waxed paper and leave to dry thoroughly.

5 Roll out the sky blue pastillage and cut out a 115-mm diameter circular plaque. Leave to dry.

6 Cut out a 320 × 15-mm strip of blue pastillage, shape it into a circle and leave to dry. This circle supports the plaque holding the shoes.

7 With a No. 2 tube and pink royal icing, pipe the design around the top of the cake and the edge of the flooded board, using the photograph for reference.

8 Attach the pastillage circle in the centre of the cake top with royal icing.

9 Attach the circular pastillage plaque to the top of the circle with royal icing.

10 Using a No. 1 tube and blue royal icing, pipe a snail's trail around the base of the circle. Using a No. 2 tube and blue royal icing, pipe a snail's trail around the circular plaque and around the base of the cake.

11 Position the ballet shoes on top of the pastillage plaque and attach with royal icing.

12 Roll out the pink modelling paste and cut out 5-mm wide ribbons. Attach the ribbons to the shoes with water, draping them over the shoes and on to the plaque, as shown in the photograph.

13 Paint features on the ballerinas faces with black food colouring.

14 Carefully remove the ballerinas from the waxed paper and attach them to the cake with dots of royal icing.

15 Make up four crescent sprays of flowers, each consisting of one miniature rose, two miniature half-open roses and two rose buds.

16 Attach the sprays to the base of the cake with royal icing.

17 Trim the cake board with silver paper edging.

Fifty Years Young

The attractive hexagonal cake, featuring sprays of acorns and oak leaves, is particularly suitable for a man's birthday.

INGREDIENTS

1 × 200-mm hexagonal cake
(page 11)
750 g pale lemon sugarpaste
(page 13)
lemon and brown royal icing
(page 13)

MATERIALS AND DECORATIONS

pattern for numerals (page 144)
glass stencil (page 22)
1 × 250-mm hexagonal cake
board
1 × 300-mm hexagonal cake
board
gold paper edging
24 acorns (page 31)
30 small oak leaves, sprayed or
brushed (page 173)
30 medium-sized oak leaves,
sprayed or brushed (page 173)
30 large oak leaves, sprayed or
brushed (page 173)
tubes: Nos. 1 and 3

1 Cover the cake with lemon sugar-paste.

2 Immediately the cake has been iced, press the stencil of the numerals on to the cake.

3 Stick the 250-mm hexagonal cake board centrally on top of the 300-mm cake board.

4 Flood the borders of each board with lemon royal icing and allow to dry.

5 Attach the gold edging around both boards.

6 Make up two sprays, each consisting of three acorns, three small oak leaves, three medium-sized oak leaves and three large oak leaves. Then make up six sprays, each consisting of two acorns, two small oak leaves, two medium-sized oak leaves and two large oak leaves. Finally, make up six more sprays of one acorn, two small leaves, two medium-sized leaves and two large leaves.

7 Using a No. 1 tube and brown royal icing, outline the numerals on the top of the cake. Then flood the numerals with brown royal icing.

8 Position the two largest acorn sprays in a crescent shape on the top of the cake, as shown. Attach with royal icing.

9 Pipe the numerals on the sides of the cake using a No. 3 tube and brown royal icing.

10 Position the remaining acorn sprays around the base of the cake, using one of the two-acorn sprays and one of the one-acorn sprays for each corner and attaching them with royal icing.

Detail of oak leaves

Hole in One!

For the golf enthusiast in the family – floodwork golfers tee-off on a green sugarpaste golf course.

INGREDIENTS
1 × 200-mm round cake, 80 mm
  high (page 11)
1 × 150-mm round cake, 40 mm
  high (page 11)
light brown, green, lemon
  yellow, flesh-coloured and
  white royal icing (page 13)
smooth apricot jam
1 kg pale green sugarpaste
  (page 13)
white and brown modelling paste
  (page 14)
brown, green and black food
  colourings

**MATERIALS AND
DECORATIONS**
1 × 275-mm round cake board
patterns for golfers (page 149)
pattern for lettering (page 148)
pattern for message board
  (page 148)
waxed paper
tubes: No. 1 and fine tooth star
acrylic square
5/0 paintbrush

1 Using the patterns, flood the figures of the four golfers on to waxed paper and leave to dry thoroughly.

2 Place the smaller cake centrally on top of the larger one, securing with apricot jam.

3 Cover the cakes with pale green sugarpaste.

4 Using the lettering pattern, pipe the message on to an acrylic square to form a glass stencil, following the instructions on page 22.

5 Roll out the white modelling paste and cut out the message board, using the pattern. Immediately, press the glass stencil on to the board. Shape posts to hold the board from brown modelling paste and leave to dry.

6 Spread a thick layer of soft green royal icing over the cake board and the top of the cake. Stipple with a knife to represent grass and leave to dry.

7 With a fine tooth star tube and light brown royal icing, pipe a shell border on the top edges of cakes and board.

8 Using the pattern for reference, paint trees and background on to the side of the lower cake with food colourings.

9 Using black and brown food colourings, paint features and details on to the golfers.

10 With a No. 1 tube and brown royal icing, pipe the message and name on to the board.

11 Attach the message board to the posts with royal icing and allow to dry.

12 Attach the message board to the top of the cake with royal icing.

13 Gently remove the golfing figures from the waxed paper and attach to the side of cake with royal icing, placing two figures at the front, as shown, and two figures at the back of the cake.

Vintage Car

Anyone who dreams of driving a 1908 Buick will be thrilled to receive this birthday cake.

INGREDIENTS
1 × 200 × 140-mm rectangular
    cake (page 11)
1 kg cream sugarpaste (page 13)
red and cream royal icing
    (page 13)
red and cream modelling paste
    (page 14)
cornflour
black food colouring
silver powder
caramel oil flavouring

MATERIALS AND DECORATIONS
1 × 240 × 180-mm rectangular
    cake board
vintage car mould
tubes: No. 1 and fine tooth star
5/0 paintbrush

1   Cover the cake with cream sugarpaste.

2   Flood the cake board with red royal icing.

3   Roll out the red modelling paste and press it firmly into the vintage car mould. Remove immediately and trim away the excess paste from the edges of the outline of the car.

4   Replace the car in the mould. Roll out the remaining cream sugarpaste to a thickness of about 15 mm. Rub cornflour on the surface of the sugarpaste and press it firmly into the mould on top of the car. Remove immediately and leave to dry.

5   Roll out the cream modelling paste and cut a strip for the name plaque (about 125 × 30 mm). Curl two of the corners as shown in the photograph.

6   Using a No. 1 tube and red royal icing, pipe the appropriate name on the strip. With a No. 1 tube and red royal icing, pipe the edging in two opposite corners of the strip. Attach the strip to the side of the cake with royal icing or water.

7   Using black food colouring and silver powder mixed with a few drops of caramel oil flavouring, paint the details on the car, using the photograph for reference. With a No. 1 tube and red royal icing, pipe the make and year of the car.

8   Place the entire moulded section on top of the cake and attach with royal icing or water.

9   Using a fine tooth star tube and cream royal icing, pipe a shell border around the plaque and around the top and base of the cake, as shown.

10   Using a fine tooth star tube and cream royal icing, pipe a shell border around the car on the moulded section, as shown.

Detail of vintage car mould and plaque

Buick 1908

Roger

Birthday Book

A handsome, book-shaped cake with moulded quill and inkwell – ideal for anyone with literary inclinations.

INGREDIENTS

1 × 335 × 260-mm book-shaped cake, made in a book-shaped or rectangular tin and built up with sugarpaste
1.5 kg cream sugarpaste (page 13)
100 g light brown modelling paste (page 14)
100 g cream modelling paste (page 14)
cream and brown royal icing (page 13)
gold powder
caramel oil flavouring

MATERIALS AND DECORATIONS

1 × 380 × 280-mm cake board
ruler or straight edge cutter
pieces of sponge or cotton wool
pattern for scroll (page 147)
glass stencil (page 22)
pattern for quill (page 147)
veining tool
tubes: Nos. 1 and 2
5/0 paintbrush
gold paper edging

1 Cover the cake with cream sugarpaste. Immediately the cake has been iced, mark the sides of the cake to look like pages by pressing a ruler or straight edge cutter at intervals against the sides.

2 Roll out some cream sugarpaste to resemble the pages.

3 Turn up two corners of the pages, as shown in the photograph. Support with pieces of sponge or cotton wool, if necessary.

4 Press the lettering stencil on to the right-hand page. Mark the scrolls in the corners of the pages, using the pattern and referring to the photograph for guidance.

5 Mould the quill by rolling a sausage shape of light brown modelling paste. Leaving a central vein, thin the paste by rolling it outwards. Using a veining tool, press lines into the paste to resemble a feather. Shape the end for the nib and set aside to dry.

6 Mix together cream and brown modelling paste to create a marbled effect. Mould the inkwell by cutting one 55-mm diameter circle from

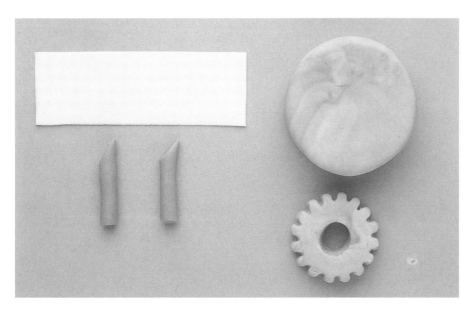

25-mm thick modelling paste. Cut a scalloped circle 35 mm in diameter and 10 mm deep, with a 12-mm diameter circle cut out of the centre of it. Attach the scalloped circle to the base. Pipe a line around the top with a No. 2 tube and royal icing, then repeat with a No. 1 tube. Paint over the lines, using gold powder mixed with a few drops of caramel oil flavouring.

7 Pipe over the marked scrolls, using a No. 1 tube and brown and cream royal icing.

8 Flood the board with brown royal icing and leave to dry.

9 Paint the scrolls with gold. Touch the inkwell, quill, letters and page edges with gold.

10 Roll out the brown modelling paste and cut out a 300 x 20-mm bookmark. Fringe the end by cutting with scissors. Attach the bookmark to the cake with royal icing, as shown in the photograph.

11 Position the inkwell and quill on the cake and attach them with royal icing.

12 Edge the board with gold paper edging.

Melody Maker

To celebrate a musician's birthday – a cake decorated with intricately piped musical instruments.

1 Stick the 250-mm square cake board centrally on top of the 300-mm square cake board.

2 Position the cake centrally on the 250-mm board and cover the cake with cream sugarpaste.

3 Place the 300-mm paper square over the top of the cake and position the 140-mm paper square and the 160-mm square paper frame in the centre. Making sure that the pieces of paper do not move, spray the area surrounding the central square and frame with an airbrush using brown colouring.

4 Remove the 160-mm square paper frame and replace it with the 200-mm square paper frame. Spray the area surrounding the central square with orange colouring, making sure that the pieces of paper do not move.

5 Using the patterns, pipe the violin, bow and four harps on to waxed paper with a No. 1 tube and brown royal icing, changing to a No. 2 tube to pipe the upright section and foot of the harp. Leave to dry.

6 When the instruments are dry, turn them over and pipe over all the lines except the strings and upright with a No. 1 tube and brown royal icing.

7 Roll out some cream modelling paste and cut out four 90 x 48-mm rectangles. Using the pattern provided, transfer the violin design on to all the rectangles. Curl two diagonally opposite corners of each rectangle, as shown. Leave to dry.

8 Pipe over the violin designs on the rectangles with a No. 1 tube and brown royal icing, piping the violin bow separately on to waxed paper.

9 Spray the four rectangles with an airbrush using yellow and orange food colourings and attach the violin bows with royal icing.

10 Using a No. 3 tube and brown royal icing, pipe a line around the inner central square on the top of the cake. Allow to dry.

11 Using a No. 2 tube and brown royal icing, pipe a line on top of the first line and, when that is dry, pipe another line on top using a No. 1 tube.

12 Using a No. 2 tube and brown royal icing, pipe a line around the outer central square. When this line is dry, pipe another on top of it with a No. 1 tube.

13 Flood the borders of both cake boards with cream royal icing and allow to dry.

Details of harp, side decoration and violin

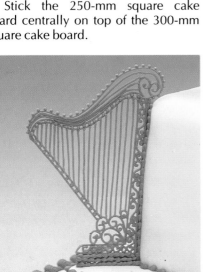

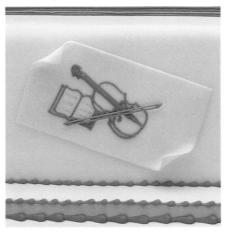

14 Stick brown ribbon around the edges of both boards.

15 Using a No. 2 tube and brown royal icing, pipe a snail's trail around the base of the cake and around the edge of the top board.

16 Using a No. 3 tube and brown royal icing, pipe a snail's trail at the base of the top board.

17 Using a fine tooth star tube and brown royal icing, pipe a shell border around the edge of the bottom board.

18 Attach the rectangles to the sides of the cake with royal icing.

19 Carefully remove the violin and bow from the waxed paper. Using royal icing, attach them to the top of the cake as shown, supporting them

with pieces of sponge if necessary until the royal icing has dried.

20 Attach the harps to the corners of the cake, using a No. 1 tube and brown royal icing.

21 Finish by piping snail's trails with a No. 1 tube where the harps meet the cake and along the base of each harp, as shown in the photograph.

An Artist's Palette

Hand-modelled fruits adorn the unusual, marbled sugarpaste, palette-shaped cake.

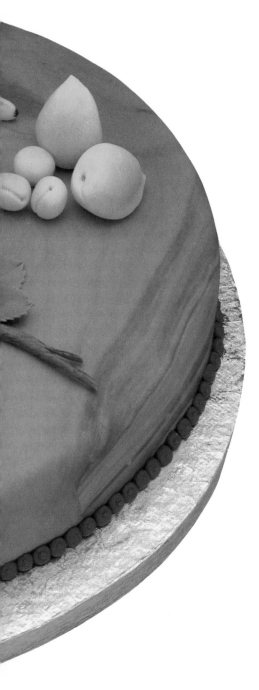

INGREDIENTS

1 × 360-mm oval sponge cake
    cut to shape of palette, using
    the pattern on page 151
smooth apricot jam
750 g beige sugarpaste (page 13)
250 g very dark brown sugarpaste
    (page 13)
500 g mid-brown sugarpaste
    (page 13)
orange, dark green, white,
    brown, yellow, red, light
    green and purple modelling
    paste (page 14)
silver powder
caramel oil flavouring
brown royal icing (page 13)
airbrush food colourings for the
    fruit

MATERIALS AND DECORATIONS

1 × oval cake board to
    accommodate cake
20-g florist's wire
paintbrush
tubes: Nos. 1 and 3
covered fuse wire
ivy leaf cutters
rose leaf cutters
leaf veiner
airbrush, if desired
pattern for lettering (page 171)

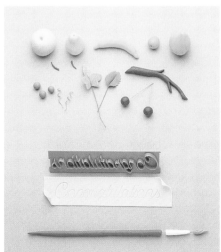

1 Position the cake on the board and coat the cake with apricot jam.

2 Thoroughly knead each portion of sugarpaste separately. Lay the different shades next to each other and combine by folding them all in half repeatedly to create a marbled effect. Roll out the marbled sugarpaste and use it to cover the cake.

3 Using the photograph for reference, mould two paintbrush handles from orange and dark green modelling paste, inserting some fuse wire into a sausage of paste before rolling it to the length and thickness required. Roll out some white modelling paste and use to make the silver-painted end of the handle. Add brown modelling paste bristles. Paint the white area above the bristles with silver powder mixed with a few drops of caramel oil flavouring.

4 Pipe beads in brown royal icing all round the base of the cake, using a No. 3 tube.

5 Using the photograph for reference, mould the fruit from modelling paste. Add stalks and leaves of modelling paste, using the leaf cutters and veiner. Either spray the fruit with an airbrush or paint it with food colourings mixed with a little water. Leave to dry.

6 Roll out a strip of yellow modelling paste, curl the corners and pipe the inscription on to it in brown royal icing with a No. 1 tube.

Detail of fruit, plaque and paintbrush

Christmas Lantern

A traditional Christmas cake, with a glowing lantern design and moulded holly leaves and pine cones.

INGREDIENTS

1 × 200 × 170-mm oval cake (page 11)
500 g white sugarpaste (page 13)
white, green, brown and red royal icing (page 13)
green, brown and white modelling paste (page 14)
yellow and orange dusting powders
gold powder
caramel oil flavouring

MATERIALS AND DECORATIONS

1 × 255 × 220-mm oval cake board
line markers
tubes: Nos. 1 and 2, and small leaf
lantern cutter
3 miniature pine cones (page 31)
pattern for holly leaves (page 152)
pattern for frill (page 152)
5/0 paintbrush
Merry Christmas mould
frill cutter

1 Cover the cake with white sugarpaste.

2 Flood the cake board with white royal icing and leave to dry.

3 Roll out some white sugarpaste and cut out an oval the size of the top of the cake. Attach the oval to the top of the cake, using a little water if necessary. Neatly trim the edges.

4 Press line markers on to the top of the cake, following the design in the photograph.

5 Using a No. 1 tube, pipe green royal icing over the curved lines.

6 Using a lantern cutter and brown modelling paste, cut out the lantern and attach it to the cake with water.

7 Attach the three pine cones to the top of the lantern as shown in the photograph, using a little royal icing.

8 Using the pattern and green modelling paste, mould six holly leaves.

Attach the leaves as shown in the photograph.

9 Brush the inside of the lantern with orange and yellow dusting powders, extending some yellow rays of light outside the lantern.

10 Press white modelling paste into the Merry Christmas mould, cut away any excess paste from the back and remove the plaque from the mould. Round off the corners of the message plaque and paint the message with gold powder mixed with a little caramel oil flavouring.

11 Using a No. 2 tube and white royal icing, pipe a line around the edge of the plaque. Paint the line with gold.

12 Attach the message plaque to the cake with a little royal icing.

13 Roll out some white modelling paste and cut out nine fancy frills, using the pattern. Set over the sides of an oval cake tin to shape the frills. Put aside to set but do not allow to dry.

Detail of decorations, cutter and mould

14 Using a No. 2 tube and white royal icing, attach the still pliable frills in an upright position around the top of the cake.

15 Using white royal icing and a No. 2 tube, pipe a snail's trail around the base of the cake.

16 Using white royal icing and a No. 2 tube, pipe a line along the edge of the board and attach the frills.

17 Using a No. 2 tube and brown royal icing, pipe lines and dots on the lantern and paint with gold powder mixed with a little caramel oil flavouring.

18 Using a small leaf tube and green royal icing, pipe some holly leaves at intervals around both frills.

19 Using a No. 1 tube and red royal icing, pipe holly berries around the pine cones and on the small leaves around the frills.

Presents under the Tree

A Christmas cake with a difference — show off your piping skills and create this delicate filigree tree, surrounded by decorated sugar-cube 'presents'.

INGREDIENTS

1 × 175-mm round cake
  (page 11)
500 g pale blue sugarpaste
  (page 13)
red and white royal icing
  (page 13)
coloured sugar crystals
6 large sugar cubes
caster sugar
gold powder
caramel oil flavouring

MATERIALS AND DECORATIONS

1 × 225-mm round cake board
1 × 275-mm round cake board
  covered in gold
patterns for oval frame (page 152)
patterns for filigree Christmas tree
  (page 152)
pattern for triple holly leaf
  (page 152)
tubes: Nos. 1 and 3, small
  straight petal and small leaf
waxed paper
gold paper edging

1 Glue the 225-mm round board to the centre of the 275-mm round gold board.

2 Cover the cake and top board with pale blue sugarpaste.

3 Using a No. 1 tube and white royal icing, pipe two parallel lines 10 mm apart around the top edge of the cake. Flood between the lines with white royal icing and leave to dry.

4 Paint between the lines with some thinned royal icing and immediately sprinkle the painted area with coloured sugar crystals.

5 Repeat Steps 3 and 4 on the top board around the base of the cake.

6 Using the pattern provided and white royal icing, flood six oval frames for the cake side on to waxed paper and set aside to dry. Paint the frames with thinned royal icing and sprinkle with caster sugar.

7 Using a No. 3 tube and white royal icing, pipe six miniature candles to fit into the frames on to waxed paper. Sprinkle the candles with caster sugar and leave to dry. Pipe nine additional candles directly into some caster sugar, rolling them in the sugar to coat.

8 Using a No. 2 tube for the outline, a No. 1 tube for the inside and white royal icing, pipe one full section and two half sections of the Christmas tree on to waxed paper, using the patterns. Set aside to dry.

9 Using a straight petal tube and red royal icing, pipe ribbons on to the sugar cube 'presents'. Using a small leaf tube and white royal icing, pipe leaves on the presents, adding a few berries using a No. 1 tube and red royal icing.

10 Stick the gold paper edging around the top board.

11 Using a small leaf tube and white royal icing, pipe nine star-shaped candlesticks on waxed paper and leave to dry.

12 Using white royal icing, attach the miniature candles to the candlesticks and set aside to dry.

13 Pipe the flames on the tops of the candles, using a No. 1 tube and white royal icing. Leave to dry.

14 Mix the gold powder with a few drops of caramel oil flavouring and paint the edges of the candlesticks, flames and leaves.

15 Attach the oval frames to the sides of the cake with royal icing, about 15 mm above the board.

16 Gently remove the six candles from the waxed paper and place in the frames centrally, attaching them with a little royal icing. Pipe three white holly leaves at the base of each candle. When dry, edge the leaves with gold.

17 Carefully remove the filigree parts of the Christmas tree from the waxed paper. Attach one half-section of the tree to the centre of the full section with royal icing. Leave to dry.

18 Attach the partly completed tree to the top of the cake with royal icing. Attach the second half-section to complete the Christmas tree.

19 Arrange the presents at the base of the tree and secure them with royal icing.

20 Attach the remaining candles to the ends of the tree branches and the top of the tree with dots of royal icing.

Detail of decorations

Santa's Sleigh

A pastillage centrepiece for your Christmas table with the festive theme of Santa's sleigh.

INGREDIENTS
white pastillage (page 15) –
   6 × recipe
white and red royal icing
   (page 13)
green modelling paste (page 14)
black food colouring
gold powder
caramel oil flavouring

MATERIALS AND DECORATIONS
pattern for reindeer (page 154)
pattern for sleigh (page 153)
tubes: No. 2, large writing and
   small fine tooth star
waxed paper
triple holly leaf cutter
fine sandpaper
5/0 paintbrush
10-mm wide red ribbon
3-mm wide white ribbon
1 × 200 × 500-mm cake board
   covered in gold
22-g wire
small pieces of sponge
foil-wrapped chocolates to fill
   sleigh

1 Roll out some pastillage to a thickness of 4 mm and, using the pattern, cut out four reindeer. Set aside on a level surface to dry thoroughly.

2 Roll out some more pastillage to a thickness of 3 mm and, using the pattern, cut out two sides for the sleigh and a 225 × 70-mm strip for the seat and back. Set the pieces over a cardboard shape and leave to dry thoroughly.

3 Using a large writing tube and white royal icing, pipe antlers on to waxed paper. Allow to dry.

4 Roll out some green modelling paste and, using the cutter, cut out and vein ten triple holly leaves.

5 Using a No. 2 tube and red royal icing, pipe three berries on to each triple holly leaf.

6 Using fine sandpaper, rub down any rough edges on the reindeer and sleigh pieces.

7 Using black food colouring, paint eyes, noses, mouths and hooves on the reindeer.

8 Using a No. 2 tube and white royal icing, pipe an outline all around the reindeer and pipe white 'fur' on the tails.

9 Cut lengths of red ribbon for the harnesses and attach them to the reindeer with royal icing, as shown in the photograph.

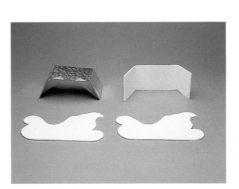

Detail of sleigh and reindeers

10 Attach the triple holly leaves to the red ribbon with dots of royal icing.

11 Using a No. 2 tube and white royal icing, pipe the lines on to the sleigh sides as shown in the photograph. Paint the lines with gold powder mixed with a few drops of caramel oil flavouring.

12 Assemble the sleigh parts using white royal icing. Attach the triple holly leaves as shown.

13 Bend pieces of wire to fit between each pair of reindeer (about 62 mm apart). Attach the reindeer to the board with royal icing, as shown in the photograph.

14 Using a small fine tooth star tube and white royal icing, pipe shells across the wires.

15 Attach pieces of white ribbon between the front and back reindeer, using royal icing. Attach the ribbon

reins (about 600 mm long) to join the back reindeer to the sleigh, as shown in the photograph.

16 Remove the antlers from the waxed paper and attach them to the reindeer with royal icing. Support the antlers with pieces of sponge and allow to dry thoroughly.

17 Fill the sleigh with brightly coloured, foil-wrapped chocolates.

Buy My Pretty Flowers!

An Edwardian extravaganza – a spectacular centrepiece that will be a challenge to creative sugar artists.

INGREDIENTS

50 g white sugarpaste (page 13)
250 g each of light brown, dark
    brown, light grey and dark
    grey sugarpaste (page 13)
light brown, medium brown, pale
    yellow, reddish brown, light
    grey, pale pink and pale green
    royal icing (page 13)
light green and white pastillage
    (page 15)
flesh-coloured, light brown,
    white, dark green, black, grey,
    green-grey, pink, burnt orange
    (brown and orange mixed),
    blue, lemon, pale apricot and
    lilac modelling paste (page 14)
cornflour
pink and lemon yellow dusting
    powders
white, black, pink and brown
    food colourings

MATERIALS AND DECORATIONS

500 × 350-mm rectangular cake
    board
tubes: No. 1 and fine tooth star
patterns for clothes and
    accessories (pages 155–158)
pattern for barrow (page 159)
pattern for street lamp (page 160)
thin cardboard cones for shaping
    ladies' skirts
figure moulds
small scissors
craft knife
cocktail sticks
dimple sponge
24-g covered florist's wire
5/0 paintbrush
anger tool
small ball tool
moulding tool
pieces of sponge
forget-me-nots (page 27)
assortment of bell-shaped and
    filler flowers (page 27), plus
    other tiny flowers, if desired

1 Roll each shade of sugarpaste into a sausage shape, then fold in half and then in half again. Gently knead the icings together to distribute some of the colour. Roll out the sugarpaste on the board to create a marbled effect. Trim the edges.

2 Using a fine tooth star tube and light brown royal icing, pipe a shell border around the edge of the board.

3 Roll out the white pastillage and, using the pattern, cut out three ladies' skirts. Place each around a cardboard cone and allow to dry thoroughly, moving periodically so the skirts do not stick to the cones.

MOULDING THE FIGURES

1 Using flesh-coloured modelling paste, mould a head and torso for each of the three ladies as follows. Knead the modelling paste thoroughly, roll it into a ball and then a thick sausage shape. Rub cornflour over the paste but do *not* put any cornflour in the mould or you will lose the detail. Press the paste firmly into the face of the mould using your thumb. Add more paste over the back of the head and firmly press the second half of the mould over it. Trim away excess paste, using small scissors or a craft knife and rub the paste with your fingers to smooth. Break a cocktail stick in half, dip it in water and insert the broken end into the body as shown and leave to dry thoroughly on dimple sponge. Insert a length of florist's wire through the body from one side to the other, leaving a short end on each side for attaching the arms and leave to dry thoroughly.

2 Mould the men's legs by rolling a sausage shape of modelling paste. Rub cornflour on the outside of the paste, cut down the centre and then place it in the moulds, pressing the two halves together. Trim away the excess paste.

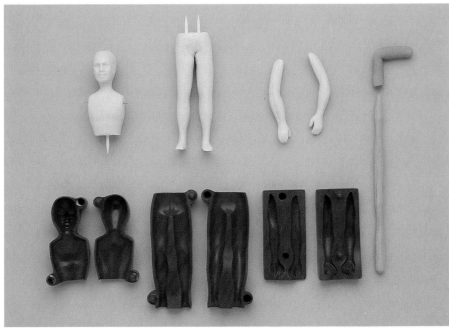

For standing, dressed figures, a skewer can be inserted in the length of the leg or pastillage may be used instead of modelling paste as it dries very quickly and is very hard. Break a cocktail stick in half, dip in water and insert both halves into the waist, leaving a section sticking out. Press a hole into the paste on either side of the stick to accommodate the cocktail sticks from the top of the legs.

3 Heads and torsos for the men are made in the same way as Step 1 (ladies), except two half cocktail sticks are inserted at the waist and a hole is pressed in the centre between the cocktail sticks. Leave to dry.

4 The children's faces are moulded by pressing flesh-coloured modelling paste firmly into the mould with your thumb and then by building up the back of the head. Insert half a moistened cocktail stick in the neck.

5 The children's bodies are moulded freehand. Roll a thick sausage shape of modelling paste and cut down the centre for the length of the legs, bending the ends to make feet. Push a length

of covered wire through the body from one side to the other to attach the arms. The completed body, excluding the head, should be about 85 mm high. Attach the head by inserting the cocktail stick in the body.

6 Arms and sleeves for all the figures are rolled and shaped separately in the colour of the clothes. Make a hole on the inside at the top of the arm to accommodate the wire and hollow the end of the sleeve to allow for the hand.

7 Make hands using flesh-coloured modelling paste, or paste in the colour of the gloves, as shown in the photograph and using a small, sharp pair of scissors. The hands are inserted in the sleeves and attached with water or royal icing.

8 Before dressing the figures, paint the faces. Add a blush to the cheeks with pink dusting powder mixed with cornflour. Paint the white of the eyes with white food colouring. Use brown food colouring to paint the eyes and eyebrows. Paint the ladies' mouths with pink food colouring, mix pink and brown together for the male characters.

Above and below: *Details of components for adult figures showing moulds for head and torso, legs and arms; children's figures and step-by-step sequence for hands.*

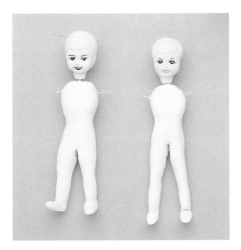

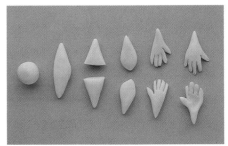

Use brown food colouring to paint freckles on the little boy's face.

9 Fill in the top of a pastillage skirt with sugarpaste. Moisten the surface and then add the lady's head and torso. Fill in any gaps with sugarpaste and smooth. Leave to dry thoroughly. Repeat for all the ladies.

DRESSING THE FIGURES

Using the patterns and referring to the photograph for guidance, make the clothes from appropriately coloured modelling paste as follows.

LADIES

1 Bodices or jackets are generally rectangular shapes which are wrapped around the torso *before* the arms are added. Openings can be in the front or back as necessary. Moisten the paste over the shoulders, pinch the edges together and then trim away the excess on each shoulder to fit. Rub with a finger to smooth. Do not paint the entire inside of the bodice with water, only the parts necessary to keep it in .place. The lapels are the corners of the rectangle folded over. The bodices of the burnt orange and the pale blue dresses are fitted into the waist. The frills inside the neck of the pink jacket are short, narrow strips frilled with an anger tool and attached to body with water before the jacket is attached. Attach the arms.

2 Cut and wrap the skirts around the figures moistening with water only at the waist and down the centre back. Any frills or markings are added immediately.

3 Make the hats, referring to the photographs for guidance. The flowers on the blue hat are forget-me-nots.

4 Add collars, capes or shawl.

5 Add buttons made from small balls of modelling paste.

6 Pipe the hair with a No. 2 tube in royal icing and attach the hats. The ribbons are narrow strips, cut and looped as required and attached with royal icing when dry.

MEN

1 Roll out, cut and attach the shoes joining the edges at the centre back of the foot.

2 Roll out and cut trousers. Attach the trousers to the body, moistening them around the waist and down the leg, and overlapping the paste towards the back. Press a crease into the front of each leg.

3 Attach the cravat around the neck.

4 Roll out, cut and attach the jacket and coat. Add modelling paste buttons and attach the arms.

5 Make the top hats. Pipe hair, beard and moustache in royal icing with a No. 2 tube and attach the top hats.

6 Support the figures with sponge and leave in a box until dry.

Detail of flower seller and two ladies

GIRLS

1 Make the hat and beret. The beret is made from a ball of paste and the pom-pom is a ball of paste cut with scissors and attached to the beret.

2 Roll out, cut and attach the boots by wrapping the rectangle around the foot, shaping it and then cutting away the excess at the back. Attach with water and add buttons on the sides of the boots.

3 Roll out, cut and attach the girls' dresses with the openings down the back. Moisten over the shoulders and pinch the edges together. Cut away excess with scissors. Attach the arms. Attach the cape collar or neck band.

4 Pipe the hair in royal icing using a No. 2 tube and attach the hat and beret.

LITTLE BOY

1 Roll out, cut and attach the shoes. Roll out, cut and attach the trousers, gathering them below the knee before adding the cuffs.

2 Make the boy's cap.

3 Attach the jacket and pockets. Attach the arms, tucking the ends of the arms into the pockets. Add the belt and buttons.

4 Pipe the hair in royal icing using a No. 2 tube and attach the cap.

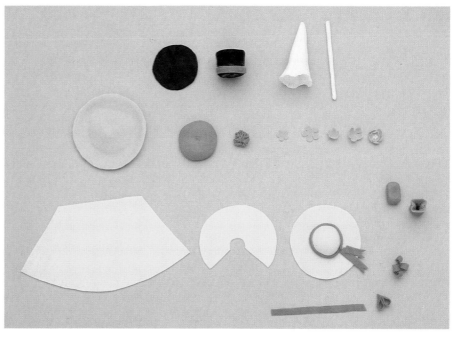

ACCESSORIES

1 Make the parasol from a hollowed cone of modelling paste, frilled at the edges with an anger tool. Roll a thin sausage shape of paste to form the handle. Attach the handle with royal icing.

2 Make the brown paper packet, held in one little girl's hand, from a hollowed rectangle of paste.

3 Make the present, held by the other little girl, from a cube of paste, trimmed with ribbon.

4 Make the basket from the scalloped circle, shaped over a cylinder or roller. Shape the handle from a thin sausage shape of paste, curved to fit.

5 Make up sprays of tiny flowers for the lady and gentleman to hold and for the basket.

6 Trim the clothes in royal icing using a No. 1 tube.

7 Attach the parasol, packet and present using royal icing. Attach the sprays of flowers for the lady and gentleman to hold.

8 Attach the handle to the basket with royal icing. Place a small ball of sugarpaste inside the basket and attach the flowers.

PROPORTIONS

The following points should help in judging body proportions when making figures:

a Place the heel of your hand on your chin and you will see that your middle finger reaches to the centre of your forehead just above your eyes. Use this as a guide when checking the size of the hands as you mould them.

b Hold your arm against your side pressing your elbow against your waist. Bend your arm so that your hand touches your shoulder. Use this as a guide when moulding the arms.

STREET LAMP

1 Roll a green pastillage cylinder, 70 mm in height and tapering from 15 mm in diameter to 10 mm in diameter.

2 Roll a pale green pastillage cylinder, 127 mm in height and tapering from 8 mm in diameter to 5 mm in diameter. Roll out and cut a 20 mm diameter circle, 5 mm thick and another circle, 15 mm in diameter and 5 mm thick.

3 Roll sausage shapes of pastillage and shape the scrolls. Leave to dry.

4 Roll out some pastillage and cut out the lantern parts. Allow to dry. Dust the sides with lemon powder and assemble using royal icing.

5 Assemble the complete lamp, keeping the lamp in a horizontal position and ensuring that all the parts are straight. Leave to dry thoroughly.

BARROW

1 Roll out the green pastillage and cut out all the barrow parts. Allow the shapes to dry thoroughly, turning them frequently.

2 The wheels are each made from two circles, with the daisy shape sandwiched between them. Fill in the gap with pale green royal icing.

3 Attach the parts of the barrow to make a box shape and allow to dry thoroughly. Trim the joins with a snail's trail of pale green icing piped with a No. 1 tube.

4 Attach the handle between the two brackets and allow to dry thoroughly. Support the main body of the barrow with pieces of sponge and attach the two wheels, using royal icing. Allow to dry thoroughly.

5 Turn the body of the barrow upside-down and attach the handle with royal icing.

6 Attach a pastillage cylinder/leg about 15 mm long and 3 mm in diameter to support the barrow, using royal icing.

7 Fill the barrow with an assortment of tiny flowers.

BIRDS

Make 11 white birds from modelling paste, shaped by hand. Roll the neck between two forefingers and pinch out the beak and tail. Mark the eyes with a sharp, pointed tool.

FINAL ASSEMBLY

Position all the items on the cake board, using the photographs for reference, and attach with royal icing.

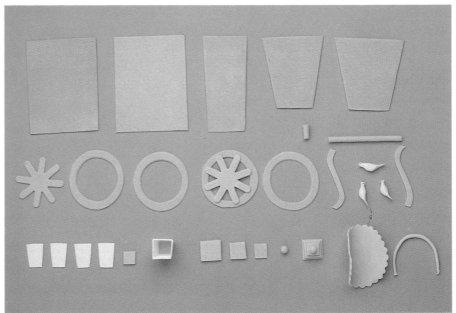

Swan Power

The mirrored base of this attractive centrepiece reflects the graceful swan and moulded flowers of the arrangement.

INGREDIENTS
200 g white pastillage (page 15)
cornflour
white modelling paste (page 14)
white, golden egg-yellow and
    black royal icing (page 13)
50 g white sugarpaste (page 13)

**MATERIALS AND
DECORATIONS**
shell mould
patterns for swan wings
    (page 161)
Easter egg mould – 150 mm long
Easter egg mould – 110 mm long
large ball tool
flat paintbrush
tube: No. 2
waxed paper
11 golden egg-yellow roses,
    airbrushed with pink (page 29)
4 golden egg-yellow half-open
    roses, airbrushed with pink
    (page 29)
13 white primulas (page 27)
300-mm diameter circular mirror
5-mm wide gold ribbon

1 Using about 100 g of the pastillage, form the body of the swan.

2 Using about 60 g of the pastillage, roll and shape the head and neck of the swan, working as quickly as possible to prevent the pastillage from drying out before the head and neck are correctly shaped.

3 Roll out the pastillage to a thickness of about 3 mm. Rub cornflour on to the reverse side and press the pastillage into the shell mould. Leave to set and then turn the shell out as soon as it is able to hold its shape. Allow to dry thoroughly.

4 Attach the head and neck to the body of the swan with white royal icing and allow to dry thoroughly.

5 Roll out the white modelling paste and, using the patterns, cut out two large wing pieces and two small wing pieces, ensuring that you have a left and a right of both. Hollow out the feathers and rounded part of each wing section with a large ball tool. Rub cornflour outside the moulds and position the wings on the moulds to dry.

6 Soften the white royal icing with a few drops of water and paint on to the head, neck and body of the swan.

7 Soften the golden egg-yellow royal icing with water and paint on to the beak.

8 Using a No. 2 tube and black royal icing, paint the swan's eyes and beak marking, referring to the photograph for guidance.

9 Position the swan on waxed paper and attach the wings to the body of the swan with royal icing. Allow to dry thoroughly.

10 Paint softened white royal icing on to the outside of the wings and the inside of the end feathers.

11 Roll the white sugarpaste into a ball and attach it to the inside of the shell with water or royal icing to form a holder for the flowers.

12 Arrange the roses and primulas in the shell, as shown in the photograph, securing them in the ball of sugarpaste.

13 Place the swan and shell on the mirror and attach lengths of gold ribbon joining the swan's beak to the shell of flowers, using small dots of royal icing.

Putting on the Ritz

A stunning design with a masculine bias – the moulded accessories are shown to advantage on the smooth white surface.

INGREDIENTS

1 × 250-mm octagonal cake
  (page 11)
1 kg white sugarpaste (page 13)
black and white modelling paste
  (page 14)
white and black royal icing
  (page 13)

MATERIALS AND DECORATIONS

1 × 300-mm octagonal cake
  board
7-mm wide black ribbon
pattern for gloves (page 164)
1 long-stemmed red carnation
  (page 25)
tubes: Nos. 1 and 3

1 Cover the cake with white sugar-paste.

2 Make the top hat by rolling a black modelling paste cylinder, about 50 mm high and 50 mm in diameter.

3 Roll out some black modelling paste to a thickness of about 2 mm and cut out an 80-mm diameter circle to form the brim of the hat. Allow to dry.

4 Moisten the base of the cylinder and attach it to the brim. Complete the hat adding a band of black ribbon.

5 Mould the cane in black modelling paste to fit across the top of the cake. Add a knob of white modelling paste to the top of the cane and allow to dry.

6 Roll out some white modelling paste to a thickness of about 3 mm and cut out the gloves, using the pattern.

7 Mark three lines into the tops of the gloves to resemble stitching.

8 Position the items on the cake, attaching them with royal icing.

9 Add an appropriate message or name.

10 Using a No. 3 tube and white royal icing, pipe large beads around the top and base of the cake.

11 Pipe scallops around the white beads with a No. 1 tube and black royal icing.

12 Finally, pipe dots around the scallops on the board, using a No. 1 tube and black royal icing.

Gazebo and Swans

A cool blue and white cake, perfect for a summer garden party, topped with a spectacular filigree gazebo and surrounded by a flotilla of baby swans.

INGREDIENTS

1 × 200-mm round cake
   (page 11)
750 g white sugarpaste (page 13)
white pastillage (page 15)
white royal icing (page 13)
gold or silver powder
caramel oil flavouring
yellow and black food colourings
blue food colouring for
   airbrushing

MATERIALS AND DECORATIONS

1 × 250-mm round cake board
1 × 300-mm round cake board
gold or silver paper edging
pattern for gazebo (page 163)
pattern for lace pieces (page 163)
pattern for swans (page 163)
sheets of acrylic
waxed paper
sticky tape
tubes: Nos. 1 and 2, and fine
   tooth star
5/0 paintbrush
75-mm diameter dome shape for
   roof of gazebo
white vegetable fat
pieces of sponge
small empty plastic jars
40-mm diameter plain cutter
140-mm diameter scalloped
   cutter
large pin
airbrush

---

1 Stick the smaller cake board on top of the large one. Trim both boards with gold or silver edging.

2 Cover the cake with white sugarpaste.

3 Using the pattern, cut out three white pastillage octagonals, Figure A, and set aside to dry on a level surface.

4 Place Figure B on a piece of acrylic, place a piece of waxed paper over the top and secure with sticky tape.

5 Use a No. 1 tube and white royal icing to pipe the outline. Using the same tube, pipe trellis work across the whole piece and set aside to dry.

6 Repeat steps 4 and 5 to pipe five pieces of Figure C and two pieces of Figure D.

7 Place Figure E on a piece of acrylic and cover with waxed paper secured with sticky tape. Pipe the lace pattern with a No. 1 tube and white royal icing, finishing the outer edges with a picot edge. Repeat to make eight lace pieces.

8 Mix some gold or silver powder with a little caramel oil flavouring and paint all the picot edges.

9 To shape the dome, lightly grease the 75-mm diameter shape with white vegetable fat and then pipe a No. 1 line around the base in white royal icing. Pipe a trellis across the dome, starting with a line right across the centre. Continue with lines across the dome about 2 mm apart. Pipe lines across in the opposite direction to form a trellis. Set aside to dry.

10 Remove the trellis from the dome shape by holding it in a warm oven or over the bulb of a reading lamp. Remove the filigree pieces from the paper by pulling the paper down over the edge of the table or acrylic square and supporting the filigree piece with your fingers until it is free of the paper. Set aside carefully.

11 To assemble the gazebo:
a Attach the three octagonals one on top of the other with royal icing, centring each one carefully. Set aside to dry.
b Pipe a royal icing line with a No. 1 tube on the second octagonal, in line with one flat face of the top one. Position one wall piece on this line, supporting it on the inside and the outside with a piece of sponge and/or a small plastic jar.
c Continue in this way, placing pieces in the following order around the small octagonal: 2 × Figure C, 1 × Figure D, 1 × Figure C, 1 × Figure D, 2 × Figure C, one side is left blank (no wall piece). Support each piece on the inside and on the outside and pipe a little royal icing at the top, where each pair of panels meet, to secure them in position. Leave to dry.
d Pipe royal icing around the base of the dome and attach it to the centre of the filigree octagonal (B). Neaten around the base with a snail's trail.
e Pipe royal icing into all the spaces between side panels, neatening with a damp brush if necessary. Leave to dry.
f Pipe a line around the top edges of the side panels and then add the octagonal

with dome to form the roof, ensuring that it is positioned correctly. Fill in the spaces with royal icing
g Attach a lace piece to each flat edge of the roof to complete.
h Pipe dots along all the joins to neaten.

12 Roll out the white pastillage and cut out a plain 40-mm diameter circle, 5 mm thick and a 140-mm diameter scalloped circle, 2 mm thick. Leave to dry thoroughly, turning frequently.

13 Position the plain circle on top of the scalloped circle and attach with royal icing. Attach the gazebo to these circles. Leave to dry.

14 Using the pattern, pipe 20 swans with a No. 2 tube and soft white royal icing on to waxed paper and leave to dry.

15 Paint black eyes and yellow beaks on the swans with food colouring.

16 Use an airbrush to spray pale blue colouring around the base of the cake, referring to the main photograph for guidance.

17 Mark the top edge of the cake into 10-mm divisions, using a large pin.

18 Using a No. 1 tube and white royal icing, pipe three loops of varying lengths from the first mark to the third, then from the second to the fourth and so on around the cake.

19 Using a fine tooth star tube and white royal icing, pipe shells around the top edge of the cake and around the edge of the top board and immediately attach the swans as shown in the photograph. Leave to dry thoroughly.

20 Position the gazebo on the top of cake and attach with royal icing.

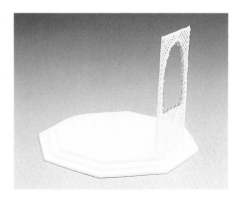

Dramatic Combination

A stylish black and white design, combining a moulded shell filled with flowers and overpiped crimping.

INGREDIENTS
1 × 200-mm square cake
  (page 11)
1 kg white sugarpaste (page 13)
black modelling paste (page 14)
black royal icing (page 13)
cornflour

MATERIALS AND DECORATIONS
1 × 225-mm square cake board
15-mm wide V-shaped crimper
shell mould
4 full white roses (page 29)
2 half-open white roses (page 29)
2 white rose buds (page 29)
18 white daphne (page 27)
28 black hyacinth buds (page 27)
30 white primula (page 27)
3-mm wide black and white
  ribbon
7-mm wide black ribbon
3 small black ribbon bows
2 small white ribbon bows
tube: No. 1

1 Cover the cake with white sugar-paste. Crimp along the top edges of the top of the cake, using a 15-mm V-shaped crimper.

2 Roll out the black modelling paste and brush the underside with corn-flour. Press the paste firmly into the shell mould, trim away the excess paste and leave it in the mould to set. Remove the shell half when it holds its shape. Repeat to mould the second half.

3 Make up two sprays of flowers, consisting of one full rose, one half-open rose, one rose bud, three daphne, six hyacinth buds and seven primulas. Then make up four sprays, each consisting of three daphne, four hyacinth buds and four primulas.

4 Attach three rows of ribbon around the base of the cake, as shown in the photograph and add the bows.

5 Place a small ball of sugarpaste inside one half of the shell. Insert the flower sprays, securing them in the sugarpaste.

6 Attach the bottom half of the shell to the top of the cake, using royal icing.

7 Attach the top half of the shell using royal icing, neatening the join with a snail's trail of royal icing.

8 Trim the crimping with a line of black royal icing, using a No. 1 tube.

Detail of shell

A Cake for All Occasions

The inscription on this classic cake with a decorative floodwork collar can be adapted to suit any occasion.

INGREDIENTS
1 × 150-mm round cake
   (page 11)
500 g white sugarpaste (page 13)
white and pink royal icing
   (page 13)

MATERIALS AND DECORATIONS
1 × 200-mm round cake board
tubes: Nos. 1 and 2
silver paper edging
pattern for flooded top collar
   (page 162)
pattern for lettering (page 171)
waxed paper
3-mm wide satin ribbon
   (sufficient to go around the
   cake twice and to make 2
   small bows)

1 Cover the cake with white sugar-paste.

2 Using a No. 2 tube and white royal icing, pipe a line around the edge of the board. Flood the board with white royal icing and allow to dry.

3 Trim the board with silver paper edging.

4 With a No. 2 tube and white royal icing, using the pattern, pipe the outlines and flood the top collar on to waxed paper, allowing for the open work. Leave to dry thoroughly.

5 With a No. 1 tube and pale pink royal icing, trim the collar and allow it to dry.

6 Secure two rows of ribbon around the cake and attach two small bows, as shown in the photograph.

7 Using a No. 1 tube and pink royal icing, pipe the details on to the board collar, as shown in the photograph.

8 Using a No. 1 tube and pink royal icing, pipe the lettering in the centre of the collar, using the pattern. Allow to dry.

9 Remove the collar from the waxed paper very carefully. Attach the collar to the top of the cake with dots of royal icing.

Pas de Deux

The unusual pink and black colouring of this elegant cake shows off to perfection the effective combination of floodwork collar and dainty embroidery with modelling paste figures.

INGREDIENTS
1 × 250 × 225-mm oval cake
   (page 11)
1 kg pale pink sugarpaste
   (page 13)
pink and black royal icing
   (page 13)
black modelling paste (page 14)

MATERIALS AND DECORATIONS
1 × 300 × 275-mm oval cake
   board
pattern for top collar (page 166)
pattern for silhouette figures
   (page 165)
pattern for embroidery (page 166)
waxed paper
tubes: Nos. 0, 1 and 2

1 Cover the cake with pale pink sugarpaste.

2 Using the pattern and pink royal icing, flood the top collar on to waxed paper and leave to dry thoroughly.

3 Roll out the black modelling paste thinly and cut out the silhouette, using the pattern.

4 With a No. 0 tube and black royal icing, embroider the top collar, using the pattern.

5 Flood the cake board with pink icing and leave to dry.

6 Using a No. 0 tube and black royal icing, embroider the board as shown in the photograph.

7 With a No. 1 tube and black royal icing, pipe a snail's trail around the base of the cake.

8 With a No. 0 tube and black royal icing embroider the design on the sides of the cake, using the pattern. Embroider four designs, evenly spaced around the cake.

9 Carefully remove the floodwork collar from the waxed paper. With a No. 2 tube and pink royal icing, pipe a line around the top of the cake. Place the collar on the cake, pressing gently to secure.

10 Using a No. 0 tube and black royal icing, pipe black dots around the inside of the collar.

11 Attach the silhouette figures to the top of the cake with a little water.

Mothering Sunday

This novel 'tea tray' is sure to enchant the recipient with its hand-painted, decorative details.

INGREDIENTS
1 sponge cake baked in a large
doll skirt tin
3 sponge cakes baked in small
doll skirt tins
500 g white modelling paste
(page 14)
2.5 kg white sugarpaste (page 13)
white, pink, lemon, lilac, light
and dark green royal icing
(page 13)
lemon and green liquid airbrush
food colouring

MATERIALS AND DECORATIONS
1 × 450 × 300-mm rectangular
cake board
frill ruler
saucer
airbrush
paintbrush
tubes: Nos. 1 and 2, and star
pattern for tray cloth embroidery
(page 165)
patterns for brush embroidery
(page 165)
spray of flowers (page 27)

1 Mix together 200 g each of modelling paste and sugarpaste and roll out to the size of the cake board.

2 Cut away the edges of the paste mixture with a frill ruler to form the edges of the tray cloth.

3 Cover the large cake (teapot) with white sugarpaste and leave to dry.

4 Cover the small cakes (cup, sugar basin and jug) with sugarpaste, shaping the spout of the jug. Leave to dry.

5 Turn the small cakes over. Roll out and cut a sugarpaste circle for the top of each cake.

6 Roll out and cut a sugarpaste circle to make the saucer. Place on a china saucer to dry in the correct shape.

7 From the modelling paste, mould the teapot lid and spout, and handles for the teapot, cup and jug. Leave to dry.

8 Use an airbrush to spray around the base of each item, as well as the handles, spout, teapot lid and the edge of the saucer.

9 With Nos. 1 and 2 tubes and white royal icing, embroider the tray cloth, using the pattern.

10 Using the patterns and referring to the photograph, brush embroider (page 21) the designs on the sides of the teapot, milk jug, sugar basin and cup with the different colours of royal icing.

11 Using a star tube and white royal icing, pipe small shells around the tops of the cup, jug and sugar basin.

12 Position all the items on the tray cloth and attach with royal icing.

13 Attach the handles, spout and lid with dots of royal icing.

14 Place the spray of flowers next to the teapot.

Masked Ball

Sophisticated and striking, this is the perfect cake for a party with a fancy dress theme.

INGREDIENTS
1 × 250 × 200-mm oval cake
(page 11)
1 kg pink sugarpaste (page 13)
black and white modelling paste
(page 14)
black and white royal icing
(page 13)

MATERIALS AND DECORATIONS
1 × 300 × 250-mm oval cake
board
15-mm half-round crimpers
pattern for mask (page 164)
pattern for lettering (page 164)
small pieces of sponge
tubes: No. 1 and large star
black and pink ribbon

1 Cover the cake with pink sugarpaste and crimp the top edges.

2 Roll out the black modelling paste and cut out two masks, using the pattern. Curve the masks slightly by supporting them with pieces of sponge. Leave to dry.

3 Roll out the white modelling paste and cut out a 'card' large enough to accommodate the lettering and piping, as shown in the photograph. Curve two of the corners upwards as shown, supporting them with pieces of sponge. Allow to dry.

4 Using a No. 1 tube and black royal icing, pipe the message on the card, using the pattern. Pipe black lines in two of the corners, as shown in the photograph.

5 Overline the crimping with a No. 1 tube and black royal icing. Pipe black dots next to the crimping around the top edge, as shown in the photograph.

6 Pipe pull-up shells around the base of the cake, using a large star tube and pink royal icing.

7 Pipe loops over the pull-up shells with a No. 1 tube and black royal icing.

8 Attach the card and masks with a little water or royal icing. Add the ribbons, securing them with dots of royal icing.

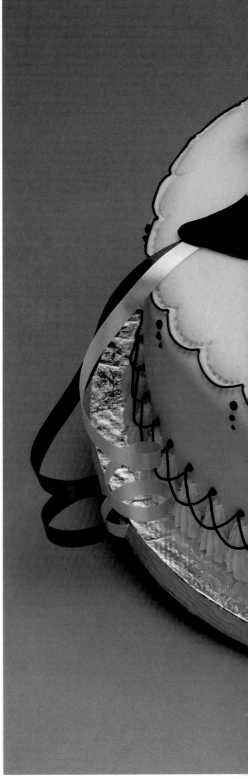

Novelties

A selection of original ideas demonstrate the versatility of sugarpaste in making decorations for a celebration party.

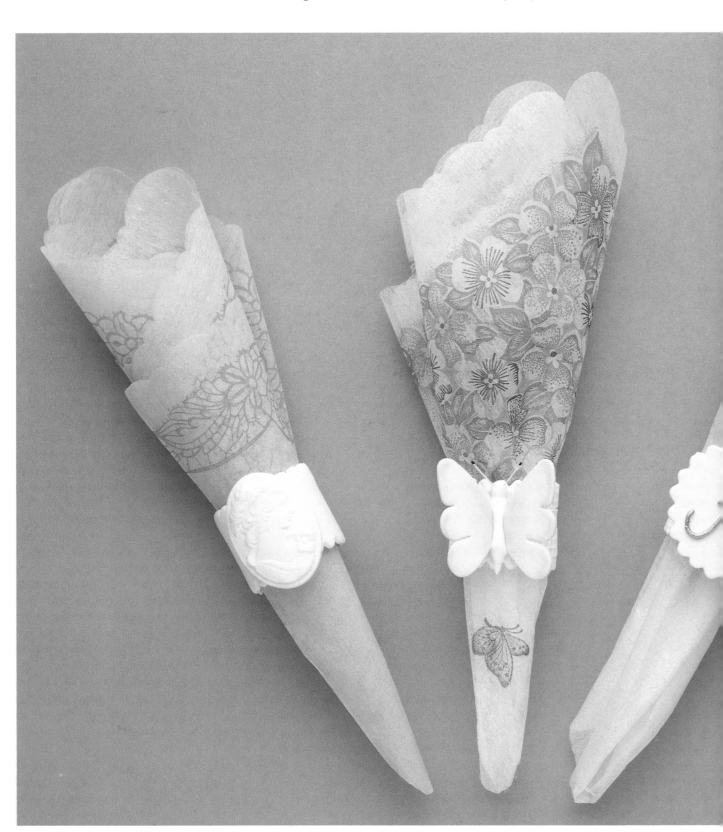

TABLE NAPKIN RINGS

INGREDIENTS
white pastillage (page 15)
white royal icing (page 13)
cornflour

MATERIALS AND
DECORATIONS
patterned or plain roller
pattern for table napkin ring
    (page 167)
pattern for butterfly (page 167)
pattern for scalloped circle
    (page 167)
frill ruler
30-mm diameter cylinders or jars
emery board or sandpaper
cameo mould
tubes: No. 1 and fine tooth star

CAMEO

1   Roll out the pastillage on a surface dusted with cornflour to a thickness of about 2 mm.

2   Using the table napkin ring pattern cut out the pastillage, using a frill ruler for the edges if desired. Immediately, mould the pastillage around the jar or cylinder and leave to dry, moving slightly at intervals to ensure the pastillage does not stick. Smooth any rough edges with an emery board or sandpaper.

3   Roll some pastillage into a ball and dust with cornflour. Press the ball firmly into the cameo mould and trim away any excess. Remove immediately and set aside to dry.

4   Smooth any rough edges with an emery board or sandpaper.

5   Pipe two rows of shells about 20 mm apart under each napkin ring with a fine tooth star tube and royal icing, to prevent the ring rolling around.

6   Attach the moulded cameo to the table napkin ring with a large dot of royal icing and allow to set.

BUTTERFLY

1   and

2   Repeat as for the Cameo.

3   Make a pastillage butterfly, using the pattern.

4   Repeat as for the Cameo.

5   Attach the butterfly to the napkin ring with a little royal icing.

INITIALS

1   and

2   Repeat as for the Cameo.

3   Using the pattern, cut out a scalloped pastillage circle. Allow to dry thoroughly. Then, using a No. 1 tube and coloured royal icing, pipe an initial on to the pastillage circle.

4   Repeat as for the Cameo.

5   Attach the circle to the napkin ring with a large dot of royal icing.

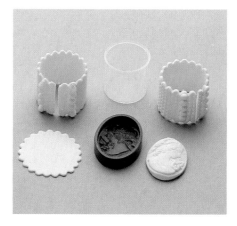

MINIATURE SHELL WITH FLOWERS

INGREDIENTS
white pastillage (page 15)
cornflour
white sugarpaste (page 13)
white royal icing (page 13)

MATERIALS AND DECORATIONS
shell mould
emery board or sandpaper
bell-shaped flowers (page 27)
hyacinth buds (page 27)
ribbon
small pieces of sponge
tube: No. 1

1 Roll out the pastillage thinly. Rub cornflour on to the reverse side and press the pastillage into the shell mould.

2 Trim away the excess pastillage and leave the shell to set in the mould until it holds its shape. Remove the shell from the mould and turn it over to dry thoroughly.

3 Neaten the edges with an emery board or sandpaper.

4 Place a small ball of sugarpaste in half of the shell. Moisten the sugarpaste slightly to secure it inside the shell.

5 Arrange bell-shaped flowers and ribbon, pushing the stems into the sugarpaste.

6 Attach the top half of the shell with royal icing, supporting it in position with a piece of sponge until dry.

7 Neaten the join at the back of the shell with a piped snail's trail, using a No. 1 tube and white royal icing.

PLACE NAME MARKER

INGREDIENTS
white pastillage (page 15)
white and a contrasting colour
   royal icing (page 13)
white modelling paste (page 14)

MATERIALS AND DECORATIONS
tubes: Nos. 1 and 2
patterns for place name marker
   and support (page 167)
pattern for butterfly (page 167)
stamens for feelers
pieces of sponge

1 Roll out the pastillage to a thickness of about 2 mm. Cut out the place name marker and support, using the patterns. Leave to dry.

2 Attach the support to the marker with a line of royal icing and allow to dry.

3 Using the contrasting colour of royal icing and a No. 1 tube, pipe a line around the marker. With a No. 1 tube and white royal icing, pipe two lines on top of each other to hold the name card, as shown in the photograph.

4 Roll out the white modelling paste and cut out the miniature butterfly wings, using the pattern. Leave to set in a corner of a box to give the butterfly a V-shape.

5 Pipe the head and body, using a No. 2 tube and white royal icing, and add stamens for feelers.

6 Immediately, set the wings in the wet body and support them with pieces of sponge until dry.

7 Attach the butterfly to the place name marker with a little royal icing.

Clockwise from top left: Plaque with Miniature Bells; Place Name Marker; Miniature Shells with Flowers; Miniature Hats

PLAQUE WITH MINIATURE BELLS

INGREDIENTS
white pastillage (page 15)
blue and white royal icing
   (page 13)
blue dusting powder

MATERIALS AND DECORATIONS
plaque cutter
2 small white moulded sugar
   fluted bells (page 14)
tubes: Nos. 1 and 2
dusting brush
ribbon bow

1 Roll out the white pastillage and, using the plaque cutter, cut out the plaque. Leave to dry.

2 Trim the bells with dots of blue royal icing piped with a No. 1 tube, as shown.

3 Pipe the clappers for the bells in white royal icing with a No. 2 tube, referring to the above photograph for guidance.

4 Brush the ends of the clappers with blue dusting powder.

5 Attach the bells and ribbon bow to the plaque with royal icing.

6 Brush the edges of the plaque with blue dusting powder.

MINIATURE HATS

INGREDIENTS
white, pink, lemon and grey
   modelling paste (page 14)
white and green royal icing
   (page 13)

MATERIALS AND DECORATIONS
patterns for scalloped and plain
   circles (page 167)
pattern for top hat brim
   (page 167)
anger tool
pink forget-me-nots (page 27)
small pieces of sponge
tube: No. 1

PICTURE HAT 1

1 Roll out some white modelling paste and cut out a scalloped circle using the pattern.

2 Flute the edges of the circle, using the anger tool.

3 Roll some white modelling paste into a ball and mould it into a dome shape to form the crown of the hat. Attach the crown to the brim using a little water.

4 Roll out and cut pink modelling paste to resemble a 5 mm-wide ribbon. Cut a V-shape out of each end.

5 Using a little water, attach the ribbon around the crown of the hat, trailing the ends over the brim.

6 Trim the hat with a few pink forget-me-nots.

PICTURE HAT 2

1 Roll out some white modelling paste and cut out the plain circle, using the pattern.

2 Lift the circle at intervals to create an undulating effect and support with small pieces of sponge until dry.

3 Roll some white modelling paste into a ball and mould it into a dome shape to form the crown of the hat. Attach the crown to the brim using a little water.

4 Roll out and cut yellow modelling paste to resemble a 5-mm wide ribbon. Using a little water, attach ribbon all around the base of the crown. Make a small bow with the balance of the modelling paste, cut the ends at an angle and attach to the hat.

5 With a No. 1 tube and white royal icing, embroider around the edge of the hat.

TOP HAT

1 Roll out the grey modelling paste and cut out a circle, using the pattern. Shape the sides of the brim as shown in the photograph.

2 Roll some grey modelling paste into a ball and shape to form crown of hat, making it about 25 mm in diameter and 28 mm high. Attach the crown to the brim with a little water.

3 Attach a hat band made from lemon modelling paste.

SUGAR HEARTS

INGREDIENTS
coloured moulding sugar
  (page 14)
white royal icing (page 13)

MATERIALS AND DECORATIONS
heart mould
ribbon
forget-me-nots (page 27)
tubes: No. 1 and small star
piped bluebirds (page 35)

Above: fluting the edges with the anger tool

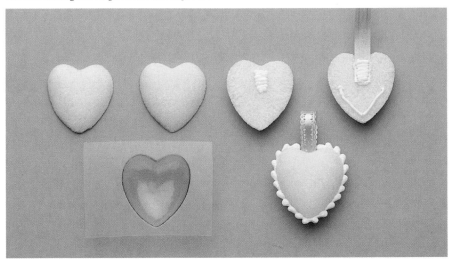

1 Press coloured moulding sugar into a heart mould and immediately turn out. Leave to dry.

2 Join two heart shapes together using a No. 1 tube and royal icing, sandwiching a loop of ribbon between them.

3 Using royal icing and a star tube, pipe a shell border around each heart.

4 Decorate with piped bluebirds, flowers and embroidery.

Left: step-by-step photograph showing how moulded sugar hearts are made

PASTILLAGE HEARTS

INGREDIENTS
white pastillage (page 15)
pink and blue royal icing
(page 13)

**MATERIALS AND
DECORATIONS**
heart cutter
emery board or sandpaper
5-mm wide ribbon
tubes: Nos. 1 and 2
piped bluebirds (page 35)

---

1 Roll out the pastillage and cut out heart shapes. Leave to dry.

2 Neaten the edges of the hearts with an emery board or sandpaper.

3 Using royal icing, attach a loop of ribbon to the back of each heart.

4 Using a No. 1 tube and pink royal icing, pipe a line around the top of each heart. Attach the bluebirds with dots of royal icing.

5 Using pink royal icing, pipe 'ribbons' with a No. 1 tube and hearts with a No. 2 tube.

The Four Seasons

This original design of the four seasons demonstrates skills in several techniques.

INGREDIENTS

1 × 225-mm hexagonal cake
(page 11)
1 kg pale green sugarpaste
(page 13)
blue, green, brown and yellow
food colourings for airbrushing
pink, white and flesh-coloured
modelling paste (page 14)
black and green food colourings
brown, pink, green, yellow,
orange and white royal icing
(page 13)

MATERIALS AND DECORATIONS

1 × 275-mm hexagonal cake
board
pattern for top of cake (page 169)
patterns for little girl (page 169)
pattern for lamb (page 169)
patterns for trees (page 168)
airbrush
tubes: Nos. 1, 2 and 3, and small
leaf

1 Cover the cake and board with pale green sugarpaste.

2 Make a stencil for the horizon, using the pattern. Spray the horizon line on the top of the cake with an airbrush and on each side, using the photograph for reference.

3 Using the pattern, mark the outline of the little girl in the correct position on the top of the cake.

4 Roll out the modelling paste and cut out the eight pieces for the little girl in appropriate colours, using the patterns and referring to the photograph for guidance on colours. The arm is rolled and shaped. Paint in the eye and boot markings with black food colouring.

5 Assemble the parts in numerical order as shown on the pattern pieces, using water to attach.

6 Using the patterns and brown royal icing in Nos. 1, 2 and 3 tubes, pipe the spring tree on the top of the cake, the winter tree on the right-hand side, the summer tree in the middle and the autumn tree on the left-hand side, using the front three sections of the hexagon.

7 Using a No. 1 tube and pink royal icing, add the blossoms (page 33) to the spring picture on the top of the cake. Pipe the leaves in green royal icing with a small leaf tube.

8 Leave the winter tree bare.

9 Using a No. 2 tube and yellow royal icing, add the pears to the summer tree, piping the leaves in green royal icing with a small leaf tube.

10 Add orange and brown leaves to the autumn tree using royal icing and a small leaf tube.

11 Roll out some white modelling paste and cut out the lamb, using the pattern. Mark the eye, nose and hooves with black food colouring. Attach the lamb to the top of the cake with some water.

12 Pipe flowers and stems in the spring picture in royal icing, using the photograph for reference. Paint the grass on the spring and summer pictures with green food colouring.

Pretty Parasol

Peach-coloured sugarpaste provides a lovely background for the various types of tubework featured in this pretty design.

INGREDIENTS

1 × 200 × 170-mm oval cake
   (page 11)
750 g pale apricot sugarpaste
   (page 13)
white, lemon yellow, apricot and
   pale green royal icing
   (page 13)

MATERIALS AND DECORATIONS

1 × 250 × 250-mm oval cake
   board
tubes: Nos. 1 and 2, straight
   petal, small leaf and drop
   flower tube or embossing tool
waxed paper
patterns for parasol (page 170)
pattern for embroidery (page 170)

1 Cover the cake with pale apricot sugarpaste, taking the icing down on to the cake board. Immediately the cake has been iced, press the drop flower tube or embossing tool into the icing around the edge of the board.

2 Using a straight petal tube and royal icing, pipe the flowers on to waxed paper. Pipe small white daisies, lemon yellow daffodils and apricot roses.

3 Transfer the parasol pattern on to the top of the cake.

4 Using a No. 2 tube and white royal icing, pipe short lines (15–20 mm) along the ribs of the parasol. Pipe one line on the outside rib, two on the second, three on the third, four on the fourth, four on the fifth, three on the sixth, two on the seventh and one on the eighth. Pipe each successive line slightly longer to give a more gradual curve to the ribs, using the photograph for guidance. Leave to dry.

5 Using a No. 2 tube and white royal icing, pipe two or three more lines on to each rib, taking them the full length of each rib. Allow to dry.

6 Using a No. 2 tube and white royal icing, pipe the handle.

7 Using a No. 1 tube and white royal icing, pipe the horizontal lines between the ribs, referring to the photograph for guidance. Allow to dry.

8 Using a No. 1 tube and white royal icing, carefully pipe dots at intervals along the horizontal lines.

9 Using a No. 1 tube and white royal icing, pipe the picot edge (page 21) of the parasol.

10 Position the flowers under the parasol and attach them to the cake with dots of royal icing. Pipe the leaves in green royal icing with a small leaf tube.

11 Pipe a small frill at the top of the parasol and a bow on the handle using a straight petal tube and white royal icing.

12 Using a No. 1 tube and white royal icing, pipe dots around the top edge of the cake at 15-mm intervals.

13 Pipe two loops between alternate dots. Then pipe another set of loops between the remaining dots, using the photograph for reference.

14 With a No. 1 tube and white royal icing, pipe the embroidery at intervals around the sides of the cake using the pattern.

Detail of parasol

Sunset Silhouette

Use your skill with an airbrush to reproduce the brilliant colours of a dramatic tropical sunset.

INGREDIENTS
1 × 250-mm hexagonal cake (page 11)
1 kg white sugarpaste (page 13)
black royal icing (page 13)
yellow, orange and black food colourings for airbrushing

MATERIALS AND DECORATIONS
1 × 300-mm hexagonal cake board
friskett (obtainable from artist's suppliers) to make stencil patterns for trees and rocks (page 170)
airbrush
tubes: Nos. 1 and 2, and medium star
waxed paper

1 Cover the cake with white sugarpaste.

2 Flood the cake board with black royal icing.

3 Cut a stencil on the friskett, following the pattern.

4 Remove the backing from the friskett and place on the top of the cake. Cover the moon, sky and water and spray the rocks with an airbrush using black food colouring. Allow to dry.

5 Using a No. 1 tube and black royal icing, pipe the trees on to waxed paper. Leave to dry.

6 Replace the stencil over the rocks. Remove the moon stencil only and spray with yellow. Replace the moon stencil and spray the water and sky with an airbrush using yellow and orange food colourings.

7 Spray the sides of the cake with yellow and orange food colourings.

8 Remove the trees from the waxed paper and position them on the top and sides of the cake, referring to the photograph for guidance. Attach the trees with royal icing.

9 Using a medium star tube and black royal icing, pipe shells around the top and base of the cake.

Part Three

Patterns for Cakes

AN ENGAGEMENT TOAST page 38

pattern for design on top of cake

WILL YOU MARRY ME? page 40

pattern for design on top of cake

pattern for lace pieces

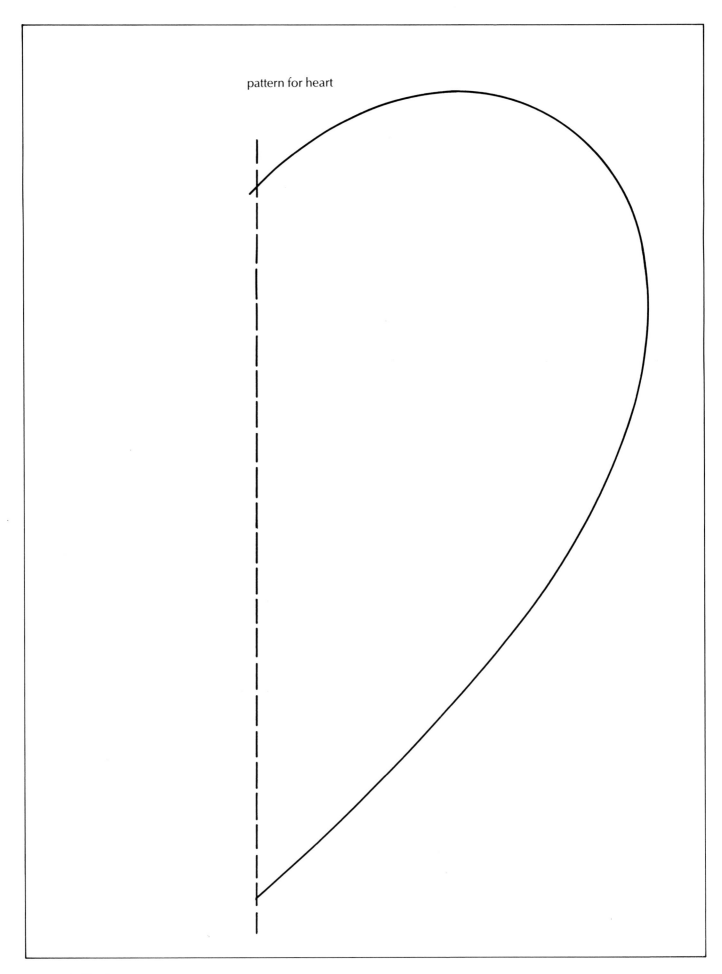

pattern for heart

pattern for bluebirds

pipe front wings separately

pattern for side of cage

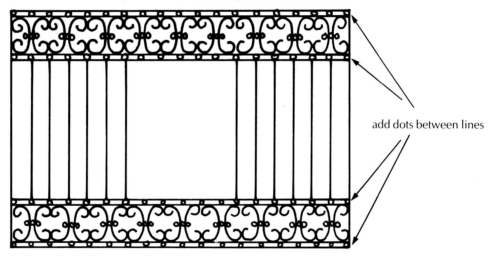

add dots between lines

pattern for dome of cage

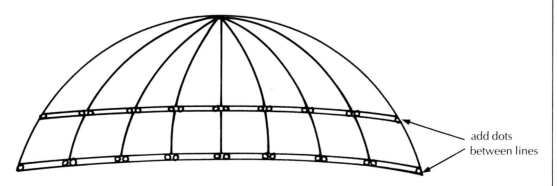

add dots
between lines

SPRINGTIME WEDDING

page 44

pattern for lace pieces

HEARTS AND FLOWERS   page 46

pattern for embroidery

pattern for plaque

HIS AND HERS   page 48

pattern for eyelet embroidery

HORSE AND CARRIAGE

page 54

pattern for horse

pattern for small wheel

pattern for large wheel

pattern for carriage filigree work

pattern for small filigree piece

pattern for carriage outline

HAPPY ANNIVERSARY page 60

pattern for ribbon insertion and three frills

3 ↓ attach frill 3

2 ↓ attach frill 2

1 ↓ attach frill 1

SILVER CELEBRATION page 56

pattern for Part A

pattern for Part B

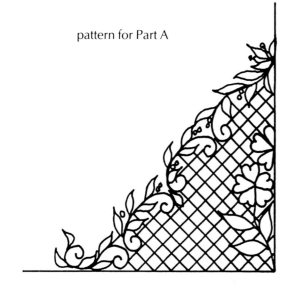
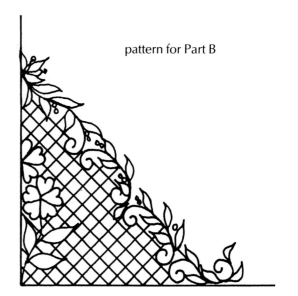

pattern for numerals

BLUE FOR A BOY
page 62

pattern for plaque

pattern for design on top of cake

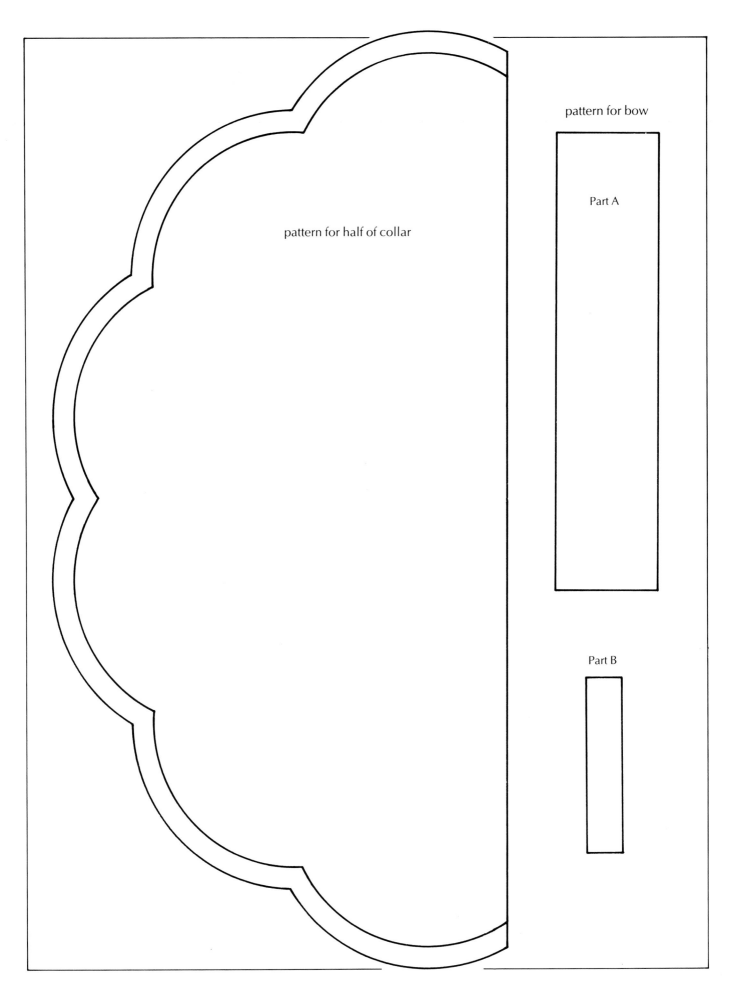

pattern for half of collar

pattern for bow

Part A

Part B

TWIN BLESSINGS

page 64

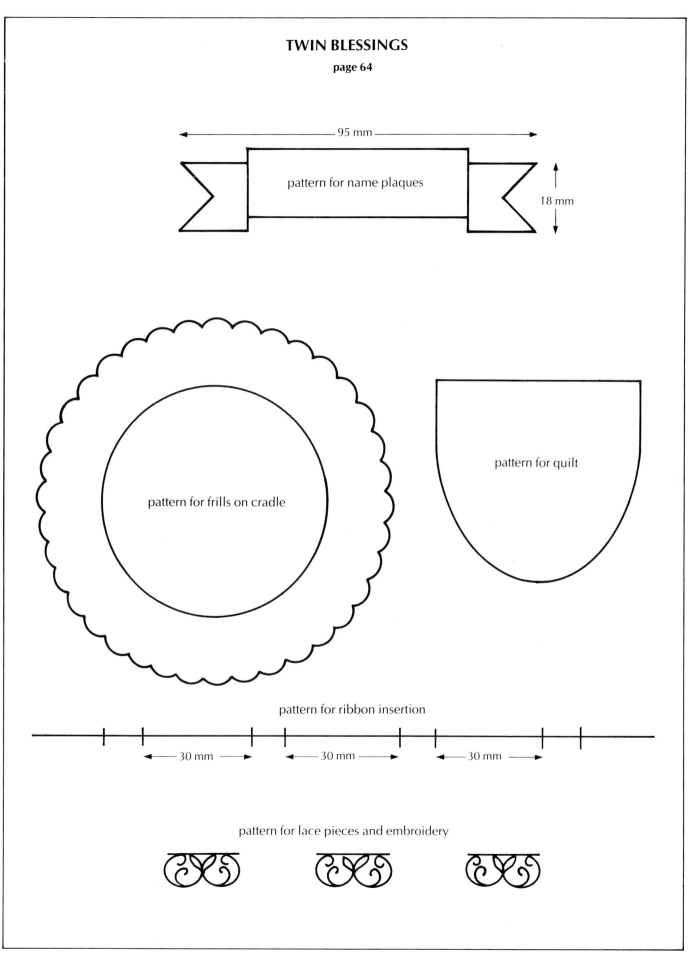

95 mm

pattern for name plaques

18 mm

pattern for frills on cradle

pattern for quilt

pattern for ribbon insertion

30 mm   30 mm   30 mm

pattern for lace pieces and embroidery

SOPHISTICATED LADY page 66

pattern for airbrush work

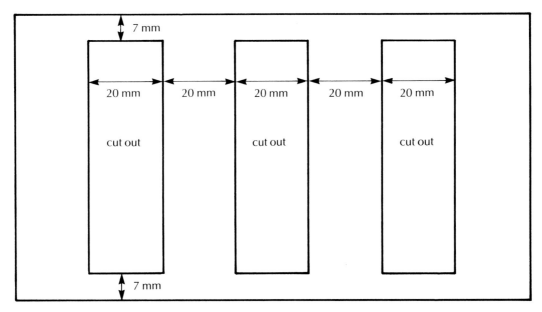

7 mm

20 mm · 20 mm · 20 mm · 20 mm · 20 mm

cut out · cut out · cut out

7 mm

make pattern long enough to go around cake

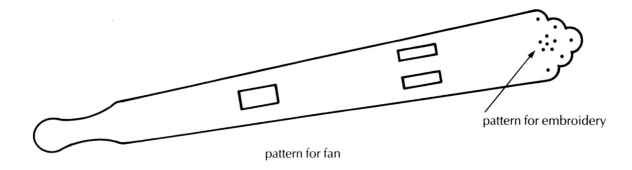

pattern for embroidery

pattern for fan

FIFTY YEARS YOUNG page 78

pattern for numerals

A BASKET OF FLOWERS

page 72

pattern for outline of basket

BALLET SHOES

page 76

patterns for ballerinas

ONCE UPON A TIME

page 74

patterns for fairy tale characters

BIRTHDAY BOOK
page 84

pattern for quill

pattern for scroll

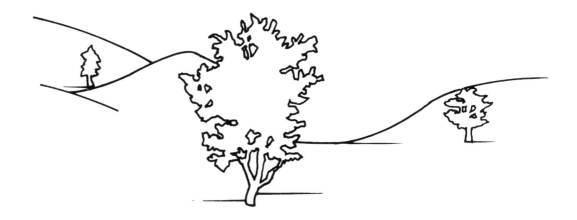

pattern for designs on side of cake

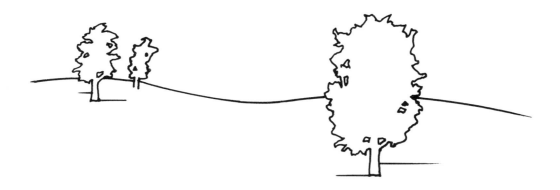

pattern for plaque and greeting

MELODY MAKER
page 86

pattern for harp

pattern for design of plaque

pattern for violin

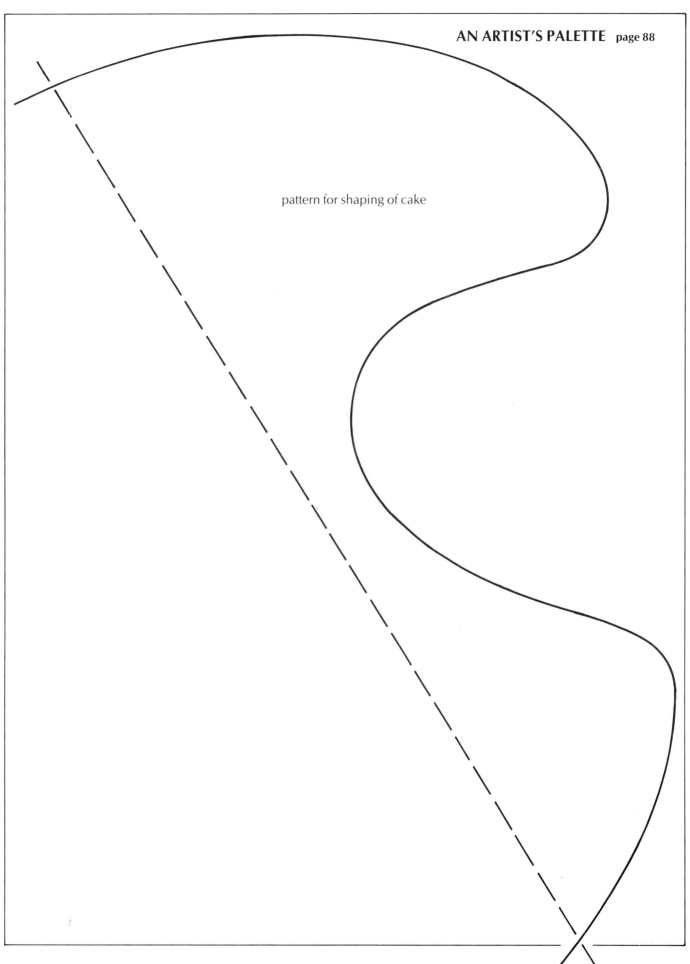

pattern for shaping of cake

CHRISTMAS LANTERN
page 90

pattern for frill (quarter section)

pattern for holly leaf

PRESENTS UNDER THE TREE page 92

pattern for filigree tree

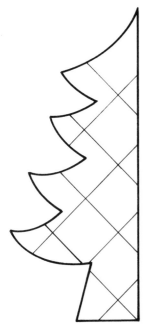

pattern for oval frame

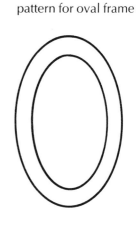

half section

full section

pattern for triple holly leaf

SANTA'S SLEIGH
page 94

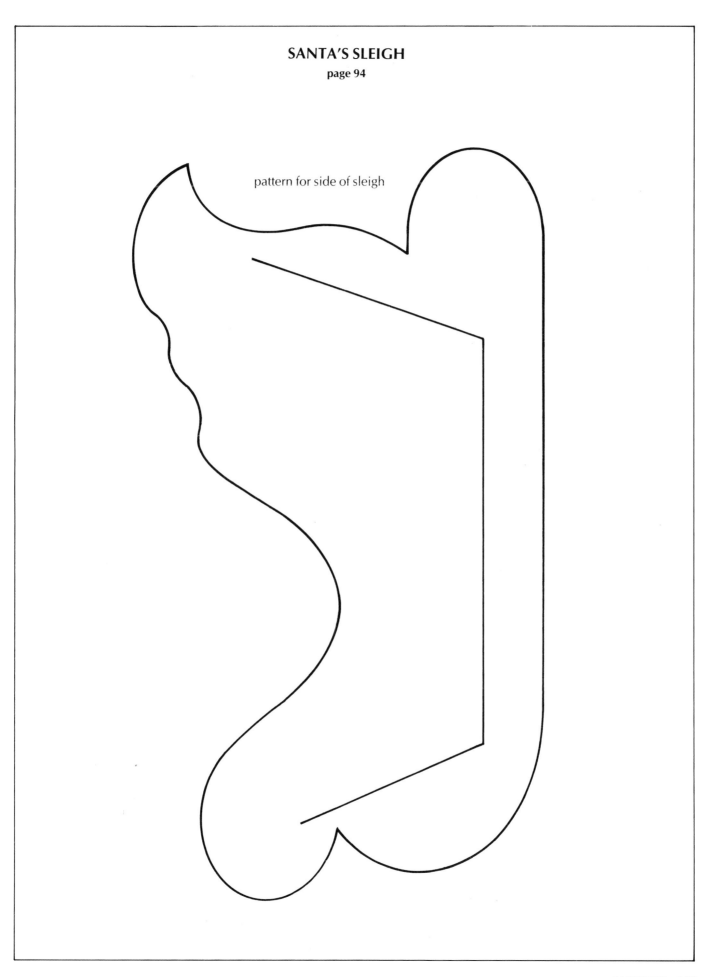

pattern for side of sleigh

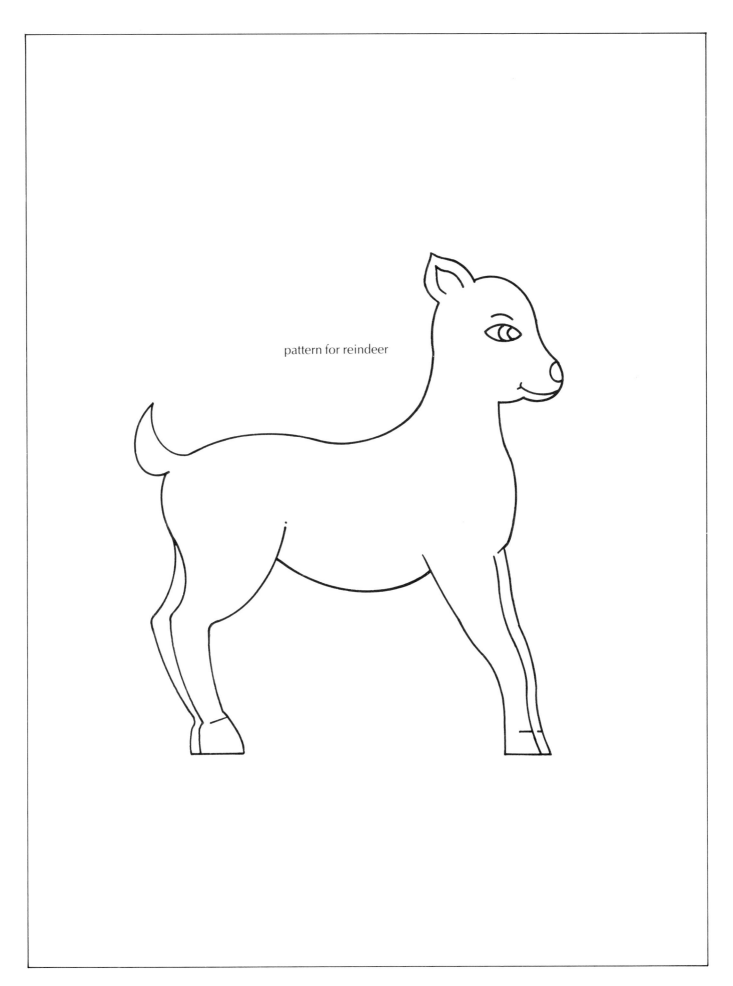

pattern for reindeer

BUY MY PRETTY FLOWERS!

page 96

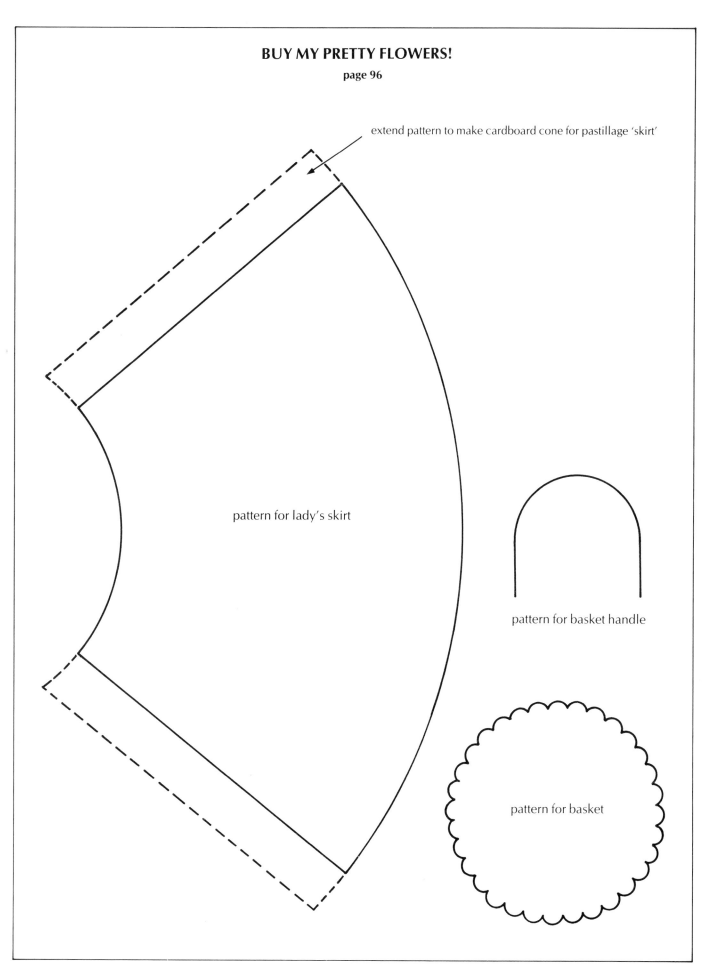

extend pattern to make cardboard cone for pastillage 'skirt'

pattern for lady's skirt

pattern for basket handle

pattern for basket

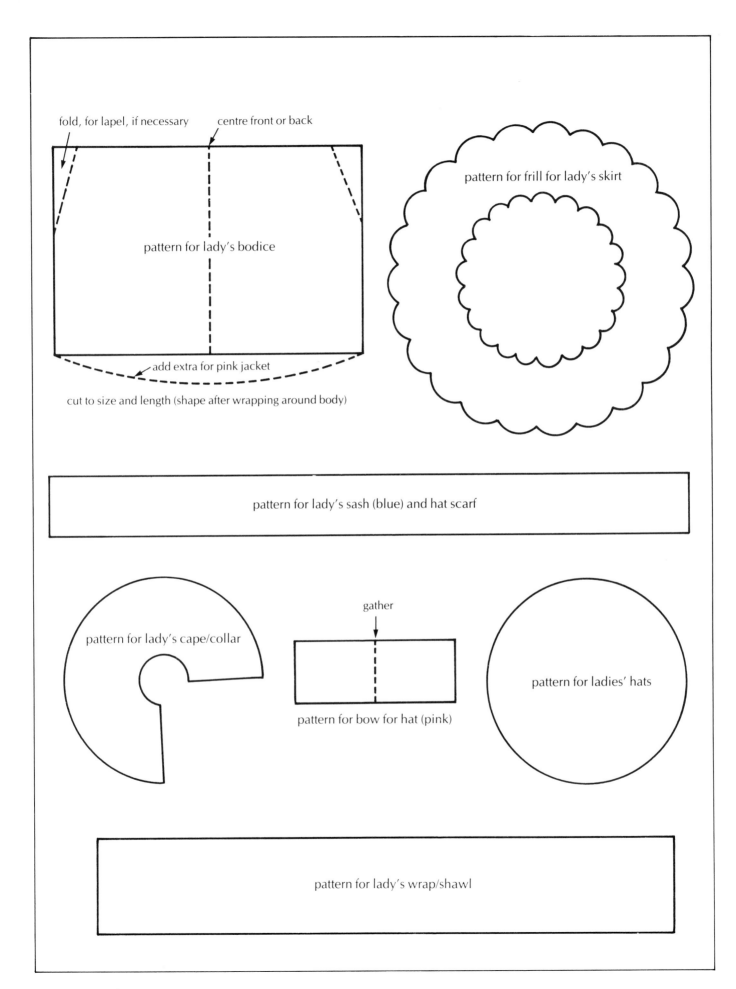

fold, for lapel, if necessary

centre front or back

pattern for lady's bodice

pattern for frill for lady's skirt

add extra for pink jacket

cut to size and length (shape after wrapping around body)

pattern for lady's sash (blue) and hat scarf

pattern for lady's cape/collar

gather

pattern for bow for hat (pink)

pattern for ladies' hats

pattern for lady's wrap/shawl

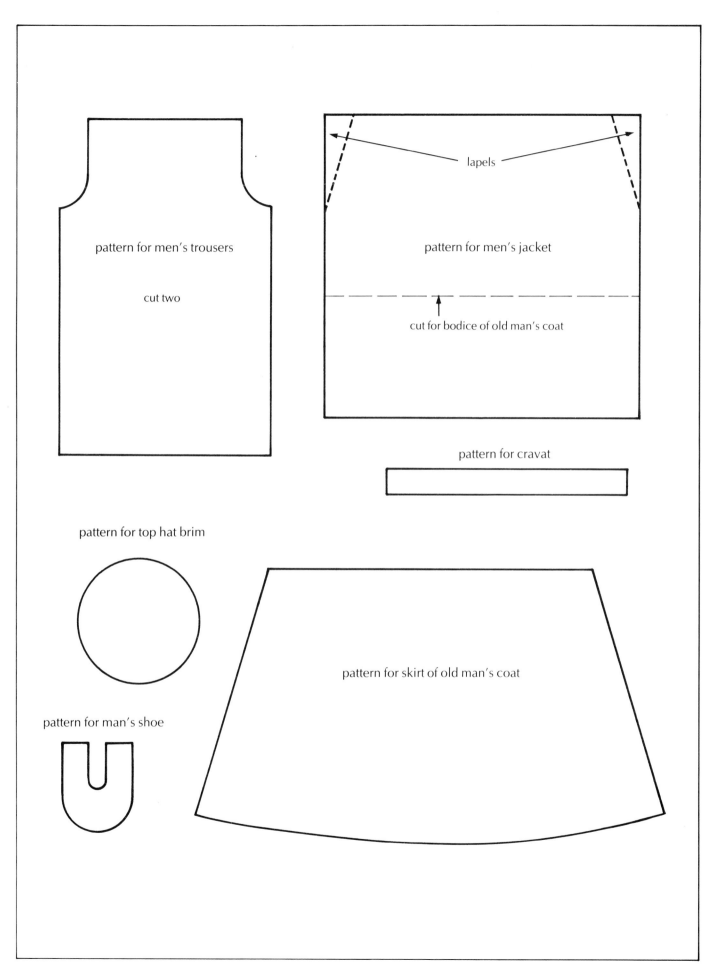

pattern for men's trousers

cut two

pattern for men's jacket

lapels

cut for bodice of old man's coat

pattern for cravat

pattern for top hat brim

pattern for man's shoe

pattern for skirt of old man's coat

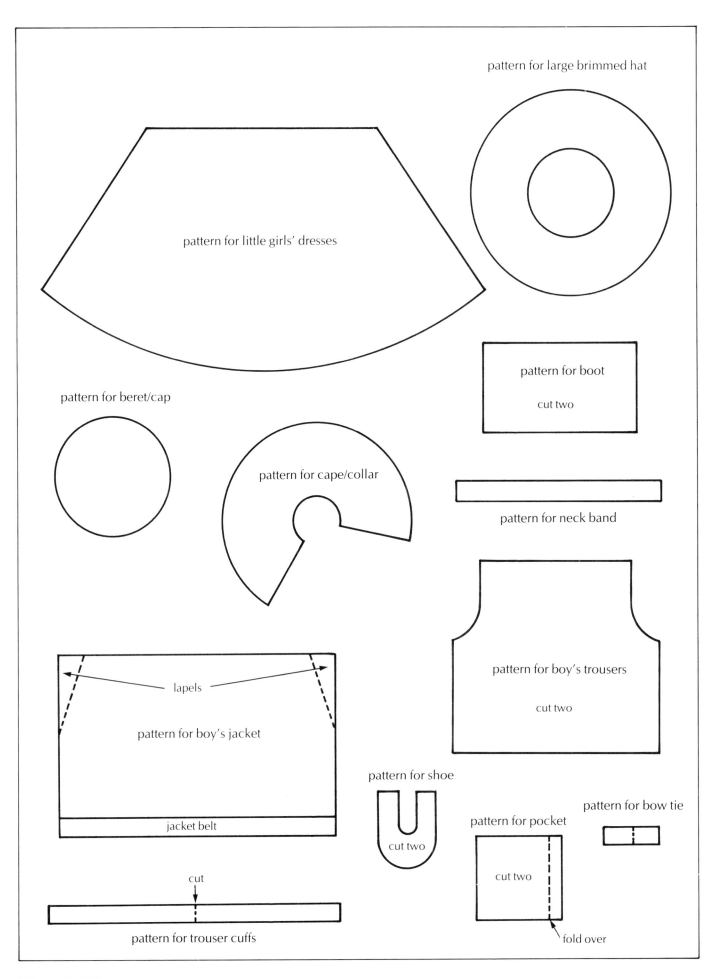

pattern for large brimmed hat

pattern for little girls' dresses

pattern for boot

cut two

pattern for beret/cap

pattern for cape/collar

pattern for neck band

pattern for boy's trousers

cut two

lapels

pattern for boy's jacket

jacket belt

pattern for shoe

cut two

pattern for bow tie

pattern for pocket

cut two

fold over

cut

pattern for trouser cuffs

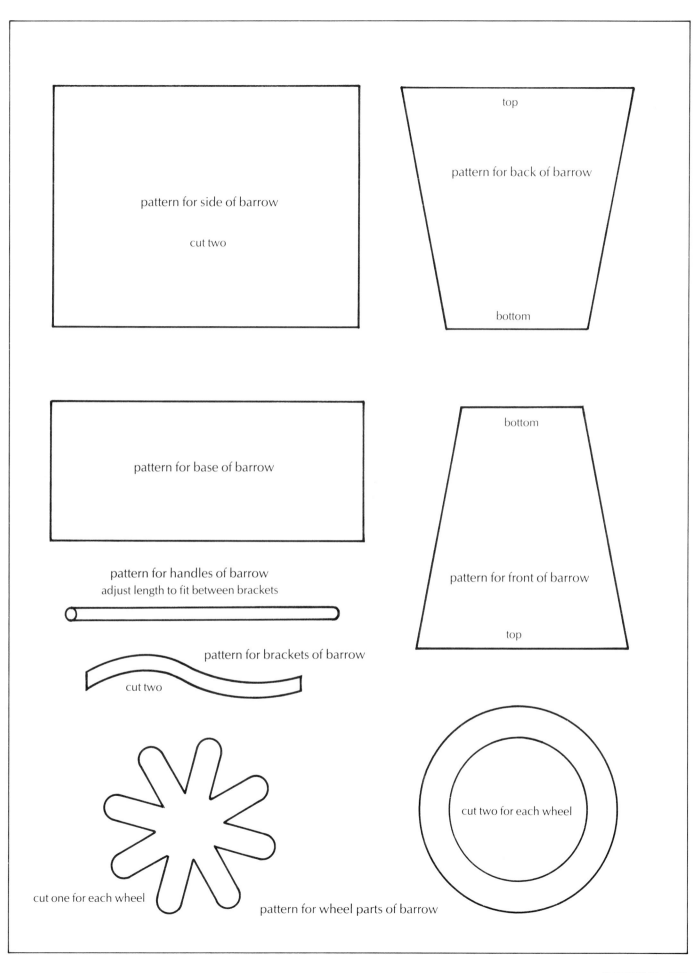

pattern for side of barrow

cut two

top

pattern for back of barrow

bottom

pattern for base of barrow

bottom

pattern for front of barrow

top

pattern for handles of barrow
adjust length to fit between brackets

pattern for brackets of barrow

cut two

cut one for each wheel

pattern for wheel parts of barrow

cut two for each wheel

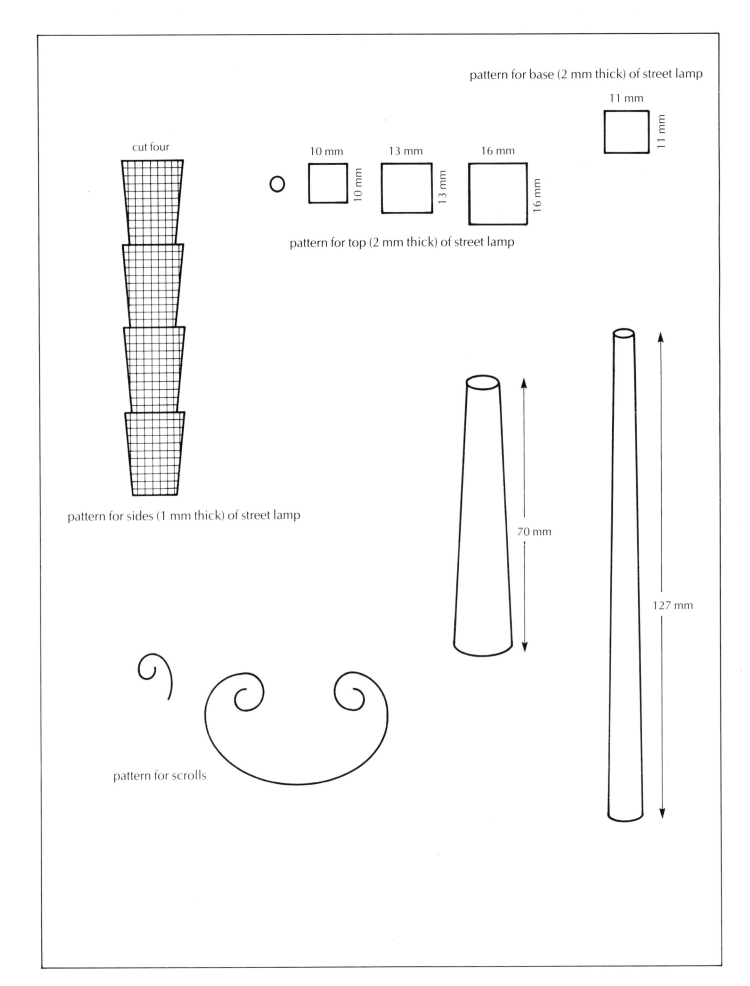

cut four

pattern for base (2 mm thick) of street lamp

11 mm

11 mm

10 mm

10 mm

13 mm

13 mm

16 mm

16 mm

pattern for top (2 mm thick) of street lamp

pattern for sides (1 mm thick) of street lamp

70 mm

127 mm

pattern for scrolls

SWAN POWER

page 104

pattern for swan's inner wing

pattern for swan's outer wing

pattern for design of collar

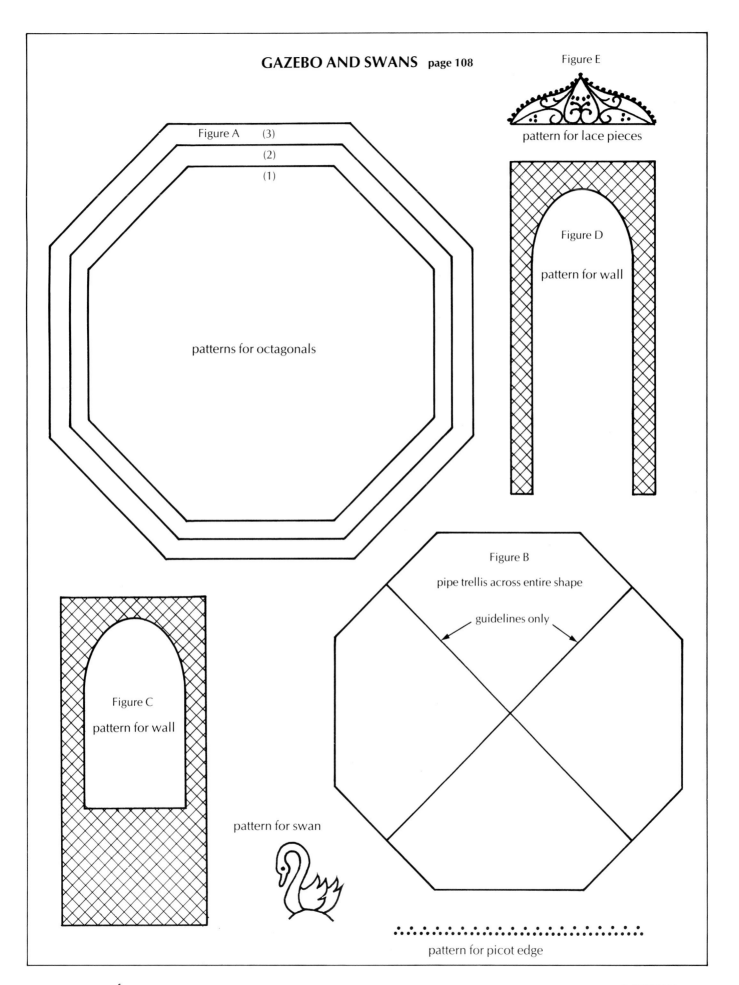

GAZEBO AND SWANS page 108

Figure E

pattern for lace pieces

Figure A   (3)
              (2)
              (1)

patterns for octagonals

Figure D

pattern for wall

Figure C

pattern for wall

Figure B

pipe trellis across entire shape

guidelines only

pattern for swan

pattern for picot edge

PUTTING ON THE RITZ
page 106

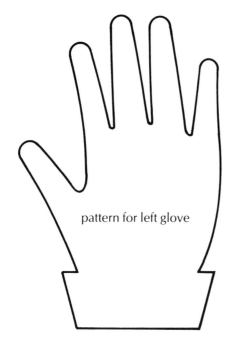

pattern for left glove

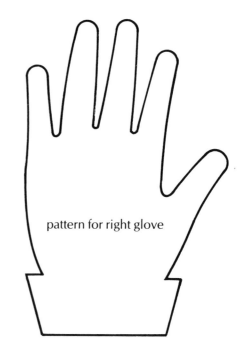

pattern for right glove

MASKED BALL page 118

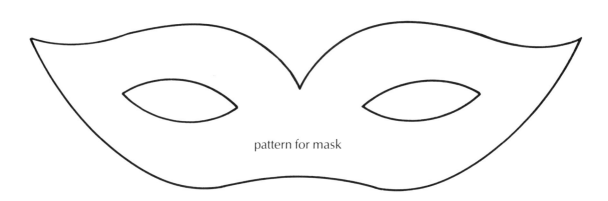

pattern for mask

pattern for message lettering

CONGRATULATION
HAVE A BALL!

MOTHERING SUNDAY page 116

pattern for brush embroidery
on tea service

pattern for embroidery on tray cloth

PAS DE DEUX
page 114

pattern for silhouettes

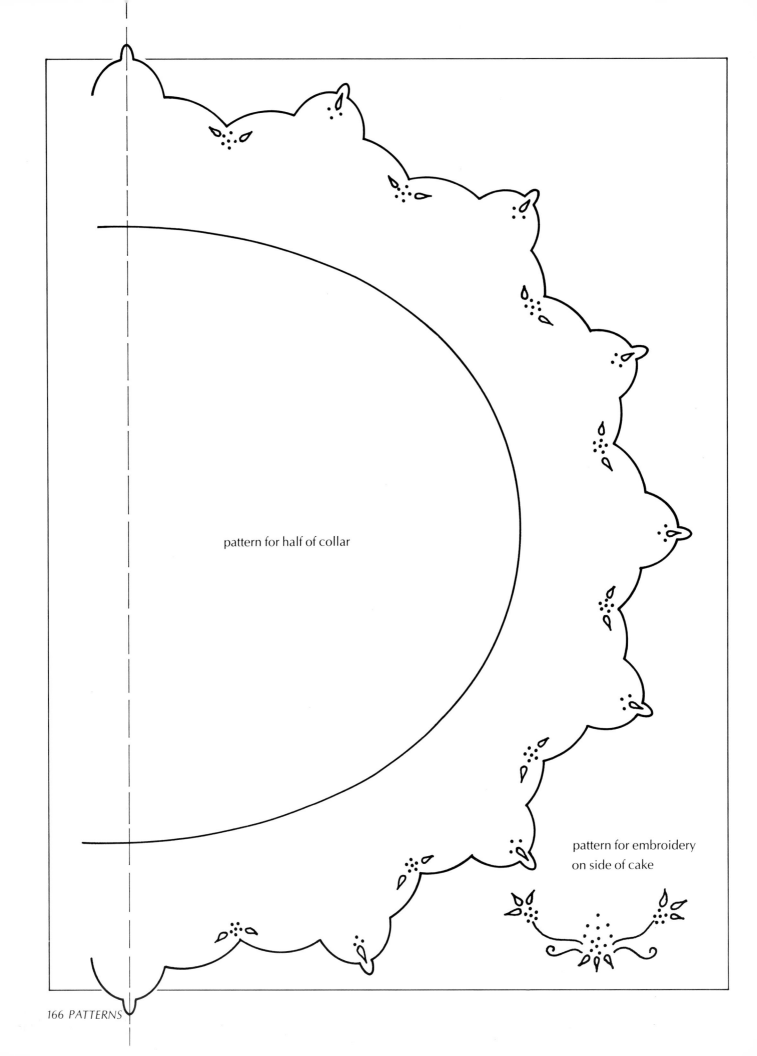

pattern for half of collar

pattern for embroidery
on side of cake

PLAQUE WITH MINIATURE BELLS

page 120

pattern for shaped oval

pattern for picture hat 1

MINIATURE HATS

page 123

pattern for picture hat 2

pattern for top hat brim

pattern for support

pattern for mini butterfly

pattern for butterfly wing

PLACE NAME MARKER page 122

pattern for outline of marker

pattern for
scalloped circle
for table napkin ring

TABLE NAPKIN RINGS page 120

pattern for table napkin ring

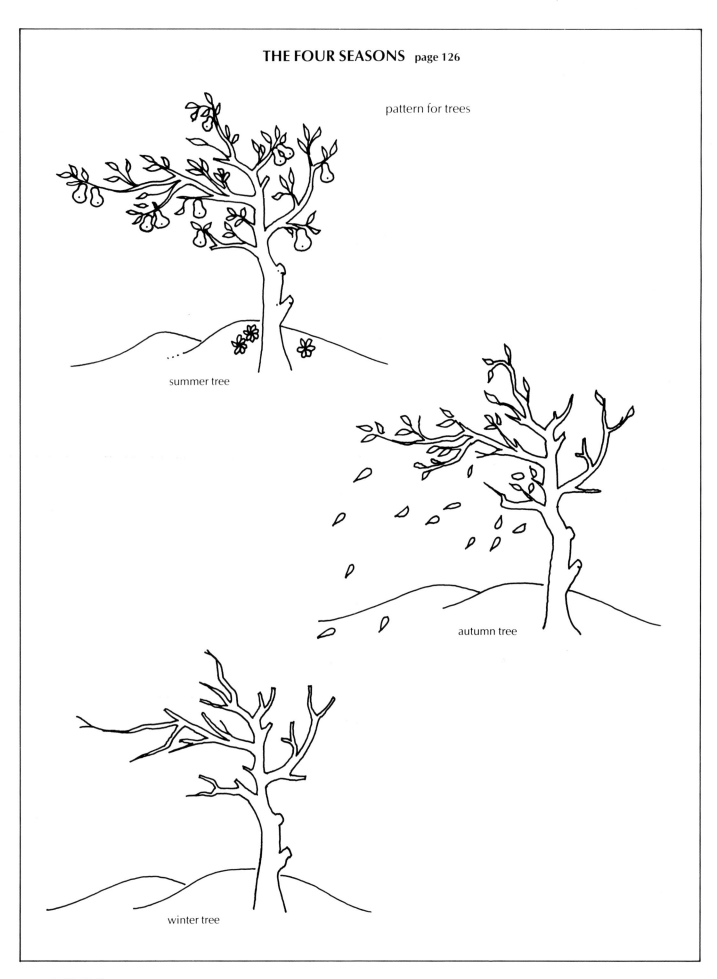

pattern for trees

summer tree

autumn tree

winter tree

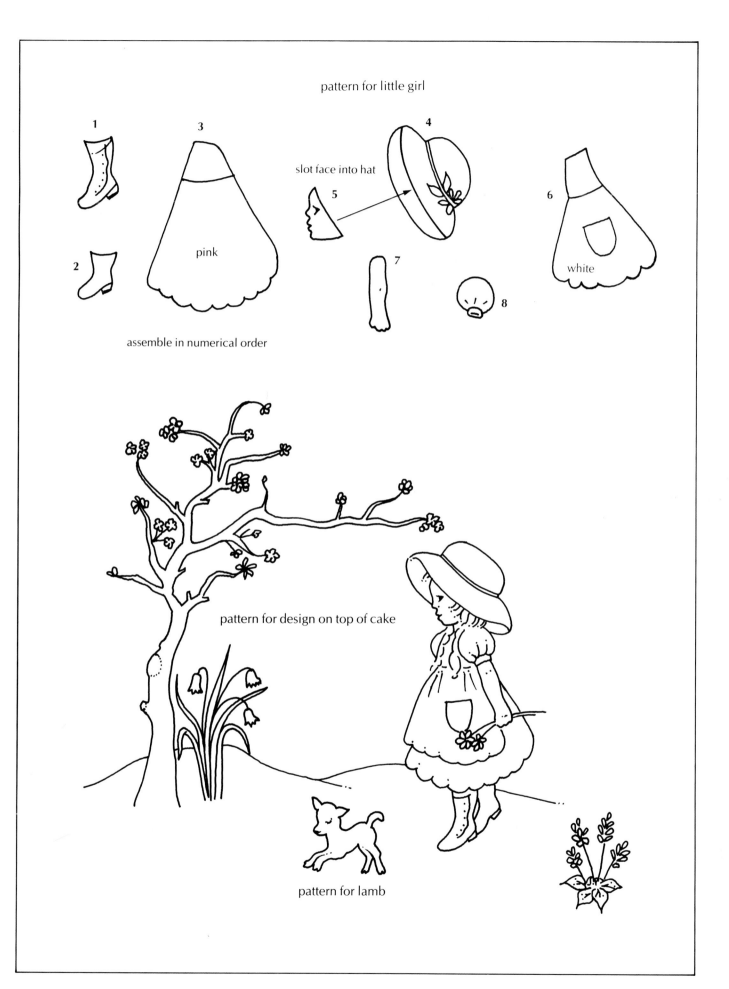

pattern for little girl

1

3

slot face into hat

4

5

6

2

pink

7

8

white

assemble in numerical order

pattern for design on top of cake

pattern for lamb

PRETTY PARASOL   page 128

pattern for outline of parasol

pattern for handle of parasol

pattern for embroidery

SUNSET SILHOUETTE   page 130

pattern for design on top and sides of cake

Inscriptions

Happy Anniversary

Birthday

Congratulations

Best Wishes

Patterns for Flowers

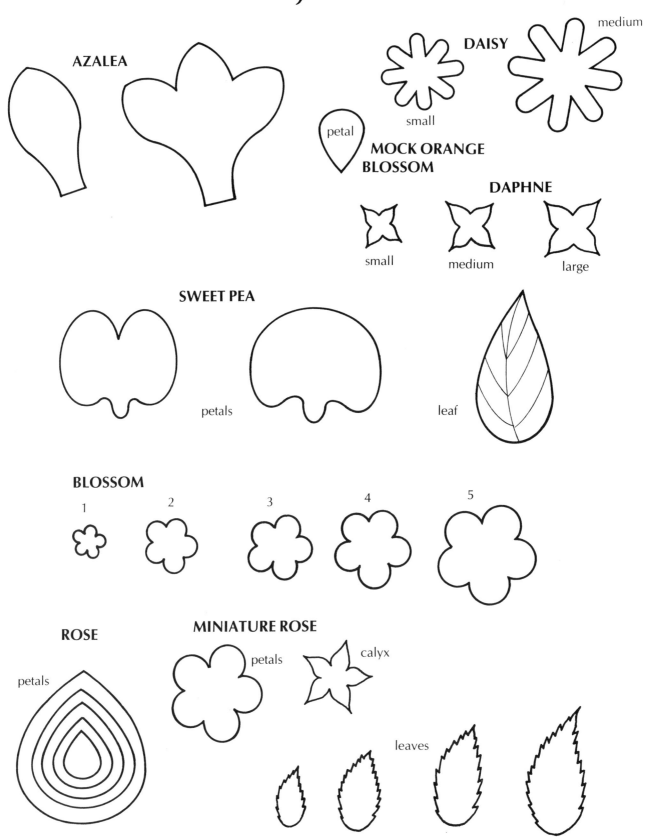

AZALEA

DAISY

medium

small

petal

MOCK ORANGE BLOSSOM

DAPHNE

small   medium   large

SWEET PEA

petals

leaf

BLOSSOM

1   2   3   4   5

ROSE

petals

MINIATURE ROSE

petals   calyx

leaves

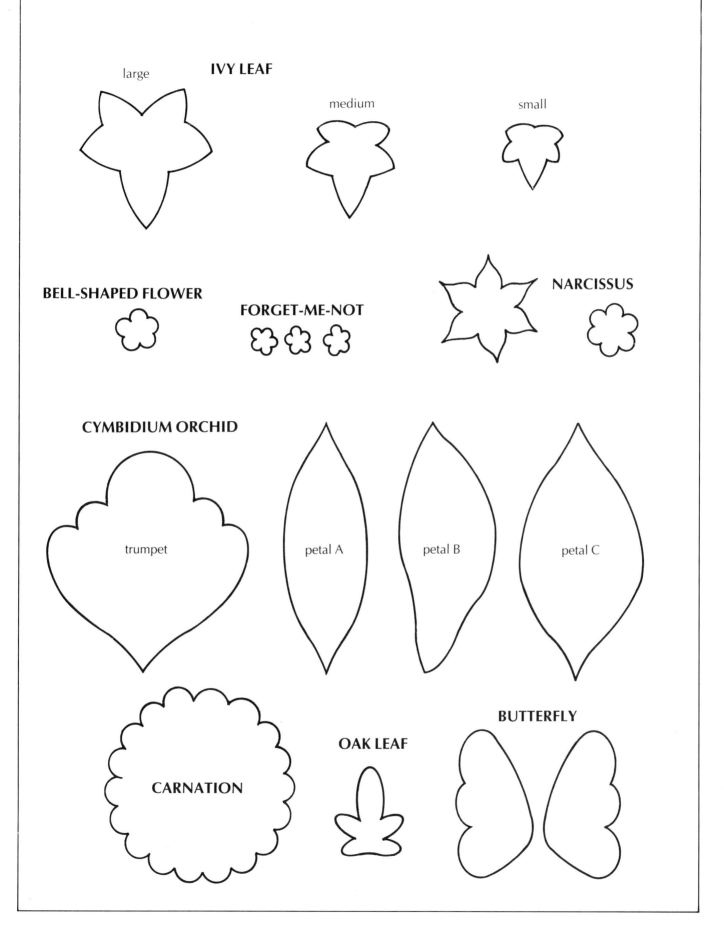

IVY LEAF

large

medium

small

BELL-SHAPED FLOWER

FORGET-ME-NOT

NARCISSUS

CYMBIDIUM ORCHID

trumpet

petal A

petal B

petal C

CARNATION

OAK LEAF

BUTTERFLY

Index